"This is exactly the book that preachers need at this critical moment in our history." —Derek Penwell, Douglass Boulevard Christian Church, Louisville

"Hopeful, challenging, raw, at the intersection of Christian faith and news headlines. Gives voice to a biblical and theological perspective usually overlooked and underreported by the media—and often in the church. An important contribution." —Sharon Watkins, National Council of Churches, former General Minister and President, Christian Church (Disciples of Christ)

"Our churches are dying because our preachings focus on proclaiming correct doctrines and dogmas. Phil Snider has assembled a talented array of ministers committed to instead preach praxis—acts of resistance to transform the church into a community which *does* good news rather than simply provides lip service." —Miguel A. De La Torre, Iliff University

"*Preaching as Resistance* is more than a tool for pastors and a beacon of hope for activists and laypeople. It is more than a crystalized moment in time that tells the story of faithful responses to the white supremacist rally in Charlottesville; the Pulse shooting; the #MeToo movement. It is about more than how to speak words themselves—it is about how we might speak, and then turn those words into action." —Austen Hartke, author of *Transforming: The Bible and the Lives of Transgender Christians*

"America is in a political crisis with many non-privileged peoples (and indeed the planet itself) at serious risk to economic, psychological, social, and physical harm. Preachers who refuse to be silent in the face of such threats will find in the sermons in *Preaching as Resistance* models that would make Reinhold Niebuhr proud for the way that "comforts the afflicted, and afflicts the comfortable."—O. Wesley Allen Jr., Perkins School of Theology

"Can preaching really change the world? Bringing together preachers and teachers who are activists and organizers—a compelling combination also found in the ministry of Jesus—this volume embodies some of the deep transformations that we need in these trying times."— Joerg Rieger, Vanderbilt University

"To read *Preaching as Resistance* is to be taught by a diverse group of saints, prophets, preachers, teachers, friends. If you are already part of a community of faithful resistance, this book will strengthen you for the work ahead. If you have found such community hard to come by, this book will remind you that you are not alone, but surrounded by a great cloud of witnesses. Either way, it is not just a book; it is balm. Read it and be encouraged." —Sarah Morice Brubaker, Phillips Theological Seminary

*For Phillips Theological Seminary*

# PREACHING AS RESISTANCE

VOICES OF
## HOPE,
## JUSTICE, &
## SOLIDARITY

EDITED BY
## PHIL SNIDER

## chalice
## press

Saint Louis, Missouri

An imprint of Christian Board of Publication

**ChalicePress.com**

Print: 9780827231597
EPUB: 9780827231603
EPDF: 9780827231610

Printed in the United States of America

# Contents

Acknowledgments      *viii*

Introduction by *Phil Snider*      *1*

**Part I: Responding to the Call**

Prologue      *11*
     When I Kept Silent, *Laura Jean Truman*

1.   Beloved Resistance (Or, the Sunday after Tuesday)
     1 John 4:7
     *Molly Housh Gordon*      *15*

2.   When to Break the Law
     Luke 6:1–11
     *Erin Wathen*      *20*

3.   Answering the Call to Prayer
     Matthew 6:9–13; Luke 11:1–4
     *Alton B. Pollard III*      *24*

4.   Everything Must Change
     Matthew 21:1–11
     *Amy Butler*      *30*

5.   More Bricks, Less Straw
     Exodus 5:18
     *Kenji Kuramitsu*      *35*

6.   Heresy of Heresies: "From Deadly Unity to Life-Giving Unity"
     John 17:20–23
     *José F. Morales Jr.*      *41*

7.   Wake Up and Stay Woke!
     *Acts 20:7–12*
     *Michael W. Waters*      *48*

**Part II: Reflecting on the Issues**

8.   Take a Knee
     Philippians 2:1–13
     *Lori Walke*      *54*

9.  Sinking: A Sermon in the Wake of Charlottesville
    Genesis 37:1–4, 12–28; Matthew 14:22–33
    *Austin Crenshaw Shelley*                                       61

10. Overcome Evil with Good
    Romans 12:9–21
    *Jin S. Kim*                                                    66

11. The Sleepless Night: A Sermon on Ferguson,
    Keeping Awake, and Jesus
    Mark 13:24–37
    *Layton E. Williams*                                            71

12. And God Hovered over the Face of the Deep:
    Transgressing the Gender Binary
    Genesis 1
    *Robyn Henderson-Espinoza*                                      76

13. Religion That Kills: A Sermon in Response to the Pulse Massacre
    Amos 5:21–24
    *Emily Bowen-Marler*                                            82

14. When Our Thoughts and Prayers Turn to Ash: Religion, Gun
    Violence, and America
    Psalm 137; Isaiah 58:1–12
    *Aric Clark*                                                    88

15. Encountering Pharaoh—and Climate Change
    Exodus 7:1–7; 8:1–15
    *Leah D. Schade*                                                91

16. Hope for All the Earth: A Sermon from Standing Rock
    Psalm 122
    *David Swinton*                                                 96

17. Dependence Day: A Sermon for the Fourth of July
    Galatians 5:13–15
    *Darryl Schafer*                                               100

18. Jesus Christ for President
    Matthew 25:31–46
    *Sandhya Jha*                                                  103

19. Nevertheless, She Persisted
    Isaiah 56:1–8; Matthew 15:21–28
    *Richard Gehring*                                              107

20. Did Mary Say "Me Too"?
    Luke 1:26–37
    *Wil Gafney*                                                        *112*

21. Deacon, Apostle, and Mother of God
    Mark 14:3–9; Romans 16:1–7
    *Micki Pulleyking*                                                  *114*

**Part III: Moving Forward in Hope**

22. Rachel Weeps for Her Children: A Sermon of Restoration
    Matthew 2:16–18
    *Alexis James Waggoner*                                             *119*

23. There Is Nothing New under the Sun
    Ecclesiastes 3:15–16
    *Jesse Jackson*                                                     *122*

24. Schadenfreude
    Jonah 3:10–4:11; Matthew 20:1–16
    *Anna M. J. Holloway*                                               *125*

25. Who Is Your Nathan?
    2 Samuel 12:1–7a
    *Gary Peluso-Verdend*                                               *131*

26. We Are "Them"
    Hebrews 6:1–8
    *Jeff Chu*                                                          *135*

27. Good News vs. Fake News
    Matthew 13:31–33; 44–52
    *Susan Russell*                                                     *141*

28. The End of Beastly Empire
    Daniel 7
    *Brian Zahnd*                                                       *146*

29. Take Me to the River
    Psalm 46; Luke 3:1–20
    *Cassandra Gould*                                                   *151*

30. The Gospel of Resistance
    Matthew 24:36–44
    *Sarah Trone Garriott*                                              *155*

Afterword by *Richard W. Voelz*                                         *163*

# Acknowledgments

When I was preparing for ministry at Phillips Theological Seminary nearly 20 years ago, I had no idea what was in front of me. My teachers provided foundations for ministry that became far more indispensable than I ever could have imagined. I don't know if any of us thought our nation would one day teeter so closely toward fascism, but I know I couldn't have done ministry these last 15 years—not to mention the last two—if not for my teachers and classmates from Phillips. It's to them that I dedicate this book.

The community of Brentwood Christian Church, where I'm lucky enough to serve as a pastor, continues to be a gift in my life. I'm also grateful for my friends and colleagues from Missouri Faith Voices, whose vision and commitment to justice is exemplary and inspiring. I express special thanks to Emily Bowen-Marler, Tia Harvey, Jim Keat, Sam Love, Darryl Schafer, Alyssa Spradlin, and Rich Voelz for making this book much better than it otherwise would be.

This is the first book I've worked on while all three of my children have been old enough to be interested in the content. Each of them—Eli, Sam, and Lily Grace—has a heart for justice, dignity, and compassion, in the spirit of Jesus. This is the best gift a parent can receive; my heart is full. I'm also mindful that my wife, Amanda, is responsible for much of this. I couldn't imagine my life without her.

I'd be remiss not to thank my parents, Terry and Ann. I grew up in the Bible Belt, where virtually everyone from my childhood equated Christianity with the Religious Right (then known as the Moral Majority). Thank you for being among the few here in the Ozarks not to make the same mistake. It may seem like a small thing to you, but I assure you, it was not.

I'm honored to work with Brad Lyons, Deborah Arca, Gail Stobaugh, and everyone at Chalice Press. As a nonprofit publisher committed to ethical principles at the heart of the Jesus tradition, Chalice resources individuals and communities so they might be part of the healing, mending, and repairing of the world. While their support in bringing this book to publication is immeasurable, any mistakes that remain are mine.

Finally, there aren't enough words to express my gratitude to the contributors in this book. It only exists because of them. My thanks to each of you not simply for making this book a reality but, far more importantly, for your faithful voices helping us find a way through this wilderness.

*Phil Snider*
February 18, 2018, First Sunday in Lent

# Introduction

*"Whatever else the true preaching of the word would need to include, it at least would have to be a word that speaks from the perspective of those who have been crushed and marginalized in our society. It would need to be a word of solidarity, healing, and love in situations of brokenness and despair and a disturbing and troubling word of justice to those who wish to protect their privilege by exclusion." – Letty Russell[1]*

*"Preachers and communities participate in resisting evil as they critique and uproot theologies that undergird it and seek to build new theologies that bring embodied justice into the world." – Christine Smith[2]*

In the wake of the nationalism, nihilism, and alt-right fear mongering that's accompanied the surprising rise and valorization of Donald Trump, many pastors find themselves drawn toward acts of resistance—sometimes even from the pulpit—in ways they perhaps hadn't considered before, at least not with the same sense of urgency they now feel.[3] It's easy for pastors to feel overwhelmed by the sheer magnitude of the task. While they may be shocked that a significant number of Americans continue to lend their support to a person—and movement—fueled by white supremacy, exploitation, heteropatriarchy, and greed, they also desire to have their own respective voices contribute to a world that's much more reflective of the love, compassion, and justice at the heart of Christ than to the arrogance, violence, and authoritarianism that's long been associated with the Pharaohs, Caesars, and tyrants of this world.

Crafting sermons that invite listeners to faithfully imagine, embody, and experience the transformation harbored in the gospel of Christ is among the most difficult of all vocational tasks. While pastors of the resistance recognize there is always much work to be done beyond the pulpit, they also know their call to preach—lived out within their respective congregational contexts—carries the potential to shape life-changing discourse in no small way. If pastors wish to resist, challenge, and trouble the problematic structures of oppression that are increasingly crashing in from all sides, the influence of preaching is not to be underestimated. Through the art of preaching—though not limited to it—communities of faith share in the kind of public theological discourses that can, in the words of Namsoon Kang,

> function in various ways as sites of contestation and resistance, of forming new religious and personal identities, and of

building solidarities. . . . Theological discourse contributes to the deconstruction of the old and the constant reconstitution of the new religious identities; to new understandings of the self, the world, and the divine; and to a new vision for an alternative world and one's commitment to a more just world.[4]

This book was put together for two main purposes: First, to help everyday pastors with a passion for justice reflect on how their preaching might meaningfully engage their congregations in times such as these. And second, to provide a Christian witness that reminds our culture at large that it's erroneous to think that all religious leaders and people of faith do the bidding of the Religious Right. The preachers whose sermons are featured in this volume do not hide behind the safe confines of the pastor's study nor the ivory tower of the academy. They may be preachers and teachers, but they're also activists and organizers (I anticipate that many of you reading this book are as well). Their vocational witness reminds us that choosing between the office of pastor and prophet has always been a false dichotomy, and one that perpetuates problematic power structures at that.[5] Their passion for justice is palpable; in a certain sense, each of these sermons was forged on the streets, amidst the people, with hopes and sighs and tears too deep for words.

The scope of these sermons reminds us that preaching as resistance is not based on some sort of Pollyanna sentimentalism. Rather, we see that faithful preaching acknowledges the realities of the world we inhabit yet at the same time invites listeners hungry for justice and truth to experience another reality altogether: the call of the kin-dom of God and the claim that such a call makes on our lives and world. This call does not come with the same bombastic flair we have come to associate with the demagogues of this world; instead, it comes through the unconditional appeal and solicitation of the gospel of Christ. This call is not rooted in dominance, subjugation, and brute power, but in Christ's saving work of justice, solidarity, and love. It breaks into space and time, causing that which exists (the principalities and powers) to tremble under the weight of that which should be (the kin-dom of God), and as we experience it we hunger for it all the more (it carries an affective appeal). This approach to preaching harbors the potential to resist the intrusive impositions of death-dealing power structures in order to make room for the transforming realm of God. It opens the conventional horizon of our expectations and leads us into different ways of being, both individually and communally.[6] From this perspective, Scott Haldeman's description of worship becomes apropos of preaching as well:

> [Preaching] provides Christians with an opportunity to leave behind—for momentary and fragile periods—the structures of inequality and violence that pervade our lives and to

imagine—and, even more, to experience—an alternative mode of being, a place and time where justice and peace are known. . . . Political organization, action, and protest will always be necessary if we desire to reform society, but we must pursue ritual action as well—where in an environment of beauty and abundance, in gathering with neighbors and strangers, in the encounter of the Holy, we know a joy that, to invoke poet warrior Audre Lorde, makes us dissatisfied with anything less in our everyday lives.[7]

One might already notice that preaching as resistance isn't reduced to simply trying to communicate ideas through speech. It is better understood—in the words of Kwok Pui-lan—as a "performance that seeks to create a Third Space so that the faith community can imagine new ways of being in the world."[8] To borrow Donna Allen's language, it is "an act of embodiment and performed identity."[9] As such, *preaching as resistance isn't merely about describing the world, but changing the world.* Preachers of the resistance recognize they have the responsibility not just to call attention to the problematic principalities and powers that attempt to take life rather than give life, but also to cultivate experiential sites of embodied transformation wherein listeners celebrate the wonder and beauty of God's justice and love. In turn, listeners go from the worship space longing to enact such justice and love, in the here and now. From this vantage point, preaching is not simply about listening to ideas about truth, but is rather about experiencing the truth and then—as St. Augustine was prone to say—doing the truth, or making the truth happen (*facere veritatum*).[10]

Preaching as resistance has less to do with trying to get hardline right-wing listeners to change their minds through the act of speech alone, and more to do with Christian proclamation that helps create and shape life-giving identities and values, rooted in community and solidarity with those crushed by the ruling powers. Preachers of the resistance recognize that theory doesn't necessarily precede praxis; rather, praxis informs theory ("from action flows understanding," as Miguel De La Torre reminds us).[11] While it's theoretically possible for sermons to resonate with those on "both sides of the aisle," so to speak, the dominant narratives within contemporary American society (especially those aligned with the Religious Right that are primarily in the service of oligarchs) are problematic—or, might I say, *sinful*. As such, preachers of the gospel have the responsibility to resist these narratives, not placate them. Resistance preaching aims to help subjugated people reimagine and experience their lives freed from the authoritarian narratives that the dominant principalities and powers wish to impose upon them. And it aims to help those benefitting from—and (perhaps unwittingly) colluding with—those powers to imagine ways to disentangle their lives from them (to repent; to be born again). In this sense, preaching is a communal act of liberation, rooted in deep solidarity and freedom. When liberating narratives of ultimacy are offered by preachers of the resistance—narratives that disrupt, subvert, and provoke the dominant narratives imposed by the oppressor—then preaching provides opportunities to experience a new mode of being, rooted in the saving work of Christ, for both the oppressed and, hopefully, the oppressor. James Cone captures the affective appeal of this mode of preaching in his book, *The Cross and the Lynching Tree*:

> [Many black ministers] proclaimed what they felt in song and sermon and let the truth of their proclamation bear witness to God's redemptive presence in their resistance to oppression. Their sense of redemption through Jesus' cross was not a propositional belief or a doctrine derived from the study of theology. Redemption was an amazing *experience* of salvation, an eschatological promise of freedom that gave transcendent meaning to black lives that no lynching tree could take from them.[12]

The promise that is evoked and harbored in the name of Christ, and the experience of its "transcendent meaning," as Cone describes, leads to mobilizing, organizing, and working for substantive change, as much as possible. But the work of changing hearts and minds—not to mention policies and communities—cannot be left to the work of proclamation alone (the call demands a response). Martin Luther King Jr. was a brilliant orator. He was an even better organizer and activist. This doesn't mean that all pastors must have the skillset necessary to excel at community organizing (in this regard it's sometimes beneficial for pastors to learn how to follow other community leaders), but it is to say that the work of justice can't be relegated just to preaching. Sermons can inspire listeners and invite them to experience another way of being, but such experiences are not the endgame. They are entry points along the way. As preaching invites listeners to reimagine and refigure their lives, it leaves them longing for the kin-dom to come all the more, so that their lives and communities might better live in to the justice and dignity that are hallmarks of it.

This is where congregations that are largely affluent or privileged must be particularly careful. All too often, well-meaning people in churches of privilege use sermonic discourse as part of their virtue signaling. They feel good about believing the right things. Or having their hearts in the right place. But they don't follow up such feelings with sustained, concrete acts of resistance. When this is the case, sermons become problematic symbolic gestures that run the risk of perpetuating power structures more than subverting them. Those who benefit from structures of white supremacy and heteropatriarchy—including white male cishet preachers like myself—must be willing to wade into this milieu far beyond the words we speak from behind a pulpit on Sunday mornings. While preaching can be transformative and sustaining—and an essential component of resistance—it's only part of the equation. The hard work of organizing, marching, protesting, demonstrating, and forging community must accompany the hard work of preaching.

When reflecting on what to preach, Thomas Long says that pastors must answer the question that cries out from every congregation, everywhere, every week: "The claim of the text is quite occasion specific; it is what we hear on *this day*, from *this text*, for *these people*, in *these circumstances*, at *this juncture* in their lives. Is there a word from the Lord *today?*"[13] What is that word, and how is it to be shared? While it's difficult to distill the precise ingredients that go into all sermons that preach as part of the resistance (such a task would be futile, mostly because oversimplification reduces multilayered and polyvalent approaches to preaching in ways that diminish their overall value), the sermons in this book—through various modes of style and structure that are irreducible in form and often reflective of particular contexts and social locations—tend to have a few defining characteristics that can be integrated into a diverse range of preaching methods that are already at work in the lives of preachers with a passion for justice.

From a theological perspective, preaching as resistance—across a wide spectrum of social locations—does at least three things well (though not always in this linear sequence): First, it compares and contrasts the world as it is in comparison to how God wants it to be (*the subversive truth of the gospel*). Such an approach can offer, as Kelly Brown Douglas writes, "a moral imagination [that] disrupts the notion that the world as it is reflects God's intentions."[14] Second, it invites listeners into another space and time, wherein the transforming realm of God is experienced and celebrated (*the transforming truth of the gospel*). Third, it equips listeners to do the truth, or make the truth happen, by responding to the call of justice and love harbored in the name of God (*the responsibility to the gospel*).[15]

Preaching as resistance is sometimes confused for preaching a particular sermon on a particular Sunday on a particular hot topic (the ill-advised "one and done" method). But instead of thinking about it from the standpoint of a single sermon delivered at a single time, sometimes it's helpful to think about the way that preaching shapes and forms community as a whole, over a significant period of time and a significant number of sermons (what is often called "strategic preaching"). A clergy colleague recently pointed out to me that the whole idea of "crisis preaching" is a misnomer. In times like these, she said, we just reel from one crisis to the next, which makes it impossible to fire off one sermon after another on topic after topic.[16] Deeper foundations must be built in order to withstand the deluge of information and announcements that flood us on a weekly, if not daily, basis. As such, preaching as resistance is committed to the pastoral work of community formation every bit as much as it's committed to the pastoral work of theological formation (the two are mutually dependent; they go hand in hand). Sandhya Jha, a colleague and contributor to this book, highlights this tension as it frequently plays out on social media, especially in the wake of problematic events that unfold on a regular basis. Following the U.S. Senate's first attempt to transfer massive amounts of wealth from poor and middle-class Americans to the ultrarich robber barons of our era (through tax cuts that negatively affect working-class Americans), she took to Facebook to write the following:

> Last week there were a lot of posts about "if your pastor doesn't mention how the tax bill hurts poor people, find a new church." In the wake of some police-related murders, I think I have implied something similar. . . . The thing is, I don't think we can keep doing this. Every week in church there is something we need to name and usually many things. Who talked about the Supreme Court temporarily reinstating the Muslim ban? Who talked about slavery in Libya? Who talked about the U.S. being the only country not in the Paris Accord? Who talked about Trump congratulating Navajo code talkers in front of a portrait of the president (Jackson) most committed to wiping out indigenous people? Who talked about Roy Moore and #MeToo?
>
> Who talked about all of it? . . . We can't name everything. But we can shape a community ready to resist fascism. We can shape a community ready to shelter immigrants as the government comes after them more and more fiercely. We can shape a community creating strategies to show up alongside our non-Christian faith communities as they come under attack. We can shape a community that creates space for the wisdom and leadership of people with disabilities and gender diversity and diversity of orientation even in the face of national leadership trying to erase and dehumanize all of those groups and people. We can shape a community that claims a role in building systems of justice that align with God's will for reconciliation, not just retribution. . . . In the face of an increasingly repressive and economically violent system of government, when we cannot name every current event in every sermon, let us be about the work of building a church that can resist exploitation and embrace community building alongside of and for the sake of vulnerable people. And if our congregations are not able to hear that word, let us build community in the places that can.[17]

The sermons in this book come from pastors and teachers who are trying their best to form meaningful community for such a time as this. Some pastors have been doing this in the same congregation for many years, while others are just beginning. It's all a process, and no individual or community is at the same place. All of this speaks to the importance of the relationship that pastors share with participants in the congregation, and the level of trust that is essential to cultivating meaningful sites of communal resistance. Pastoral awareness and sensitivity is a key component to building community. And building community is a key component to care and well-being, especially when despots rule with dictatorial aims.

The point of sharing the following sermons isn't for them to be replicated word for word in another setting (good preaching is too contextual for that), but to provide a sense of how various pastors draw on the rhetorical power of Christian proclamation in order to cultivate sites of communal resistance, right where they are, even if the powers and principalities don't change (as the Bible well attests, healing pockets of the kin-dom of God can still be experienced in empire, even—especially—as imperial powers try to snuff them out). These sermons highlight the shape and scope of preaching that not only resists, challenges, and troubles the problematic structures of authoritarianism and oppression crashing in from all sides, but also ones that invite listeners to experience the transformation, possibility, and hope stirring in the gospel of Christ. They demonstrate how preaching as resistance can be incorporated into a wide variety of social contexts and preaching styles. I included several sermons preached in the Bible Belt in order to demonstrate that preaching as resistance isn't relegated to big steeple churches in big cities in blue states. Rather, it's taking place everywhere, including small towns across the heartland, where it's not uncommon for parishioners to pass Confederate battle flags waving high in the air on their way to worship. Our world needs to be saved, and pastors are called to witness to God's saving work in Christ. Not just in blue states, but in red and purple ones too.

In full disclosure, I must admit from the outset that I'm not necessarily a big fan of sermon collections that only feature contributions from famous preachers who spend most of their vocational life on the speaking circuit. I wanted to show readers that preaching as resistance is not relegated to the big names in the big conferences, but is taking place among everyday pastors in everyday congregations. It's not that there isn't a place for conference preaching (one of the things I enjoy the most is listening to expert homileticians at the top of their game, whether in the classroom or the convention center). I'm just convinced that the most vital Christian preaching going on today quietly takes place week after week in local congregations, by everyday pastors committed to the hard work of justice and transformation in their particular contexts and communities. The bulk of the sermons in this book follow suit. Most were delivered in the trenches, Sunday after Sunday, week after week, among pastors and listeners who not only share a relationship but also a hunger for a transforming word of hope. That's not to say that Christian proclamation offered by pastors and leaders outside the context of a liturgical setting isn't vital to the work of resistance. It certainly is. Meaningful public theological discourse that harbors possibilities for transformation takes place at demonstrations, marches, protests, and numerous other venues, including in books and on social media. These can be essential sites of resistance.[18] However, the focus in this book, for the most part, is on preaching as resistance within a liturgical setting. This stems from the conviction that the worship space can become an essential site of resistance and that pastors need to think through the ways their preaching might contribute to it. But it doesn't mean that preachers should consider the liturgical setting to be the only place where public Christian proclamation is part of the work of resistance.

I initially planned to publish sermons that were preached immediately after Trump took office, but it became more and more clear that dynamics surrounding his ascendency reached much deeper than his campaign alone, and would continue to play out throughout his presidency and beyond.[19] Sermons in this book therefore touch on numerous subjects that may be associated with the Trump brand but are not confined to it, including but not limited to the assault on epistemology and truth (fake news, alternative facts), racism (the alt-right, Colin Kaepernick, Black Lives Matter), classism (health care, labor and tax policies, free market fundamentalism), nativism (the wall and the ban on immigrants), militarism (building the nuclear arsenal, the worship of military-grade weaponry among the populace and the NRA), nationalism and dominionism (America as a Christian nation, the supposedly Christian subjugation and degradation of the environment), sexism and the #MeToo moment (evangelical justification for Bill O'Reilly and Roy Moore, not to mention the infamous *Access Hollywood* tape), homophobia and transphobia (discrimination in the name of "freedom of religion," changes in military treatment of LGBTQ+ persons), and many more (this list is hardly comprehensive of the subject matter in this book).[20] Although Trump is the chief representative of the straight-white-cis-patriarchal power structures that no small number of Americans desire to maintain, it's important to point out that he's not the cause of this desire, but the mere symbol of it. As Trevor Noah summarized in one of his stand-up comedy routines, "Donald Trump didn't make America racist; racism made Donald Trump." Indeed, the rise of the alt-right is nothing new; it's just the explicit expression of the racism and misogyny that has been the underbelly of the Religious Right for decades (let's recall that the Religious Right was originally founded to fight integration and keep white men in power, well before Fox News was on the air).[21] The legal issues surrounding President Trump may keep him from filling out his term, but make no mistake about it: the dynamics that gave rise to his presidency will remain, which means preachers of the gospel will continue to have the responsibility to resist, challenge, and trouble all principalities and powers that are in the business of taking life rather than saving it. For now, and a long time to come.

To be sure, the call to preach isn't for the faint of heart, in this time or any other. The prophets and sages from years past remind us that speaking truth to power isn't about accolades or rewards—it's about being faithful to the gospel, even and especially when it is risky, vulnerable business. We don't preach because we're guaranteed a certain outcome; we preach out of faithfulness to the claim the kin-dom of God makes on our lives. And as we do this within community, we hope to find the courage and strength to go on, trusting that Christ's love is stronger than any force that tries to contain it. Indeed, when demagogues are on the throne (or in the White House), the weakness of Christ may be the only thing strong enough to save us.[22]

[1]Letty Russell, *Church in the Round: Feminist Interpretation of the Church* (Louisville: Westminster John Knox Press, 1993), 139.

[2]Christine Smith, *Preaching as Weeping, Confession, and Resistance: Radical Responses to Radical Evil* (Louisville: Westminster John Knox Press, 1992), 9.

[3]For the most part, this dynamic is more pronounced among white-hetero-male-cisgender pastors who've historically benefitted from prevailing societal power structures. It's not that pastors from historically marginalized communities don't also feel a major sense of urgency for such a time as this, but, generally speaking, this realization isn't nearly as new to them. Preaching as resistance has a pedigree at least as ancient as St. Paul, and has long been a primary mode of sermonic discourse among the marginalized in the United States. The rise of Trump may amplify the racism and misogyny that runs deep in our country, but it's been in the DNA of the United States since its inception, and preachers have long been responding to it.

[4]Namsoon Kang, *Cosmopolitan Theology: Reconstituting Planetary Hospitality, Neighbor-Love, and Solidarity in an Uneven World* (St. Louis: Chalice, 2013), 7–8.

[5]See especially Nora Tisdale's *Prophetic Preaching: A Pastoral Approach* and Kenyatta Gilbert's *The Journey and Promise of African-American Preaching.*

[6]According to Smith, as an act of public theological naming, preaching discloses and articulates "the truths about our present human existence. It is an act of bringing new reality into being, an act of creation. It is also an act of redeeming and transforming reality, an act of shattering illusions and cracking open limited perspectives. It is nothing less than the interpretation of our present world and an invitation to build a profoundly different world." Smith, *Preaching as Weeping, Confession, and Resistance,* 2.

[7]As quoted on his faculty page at Chicago Theological Seminary, https://www.ctschicago.edu/people/w-scott-haldeman/.

[8]See Kwok Pui-lan, "Postcolonial Preaching in Intercultural Contexts," Homiletic 40, no. 1, 2015, doi:10.15695/hmltc.v40i1.4117.

[9]Donna E. Allen, *Toward a Womanist Homiletic: Katie Cannon, Alice Walker, and Emancipatory Proclamation* (New York: Peter Lang Publishing, 2013), 6.

[10]For an introduction to what Augustine meant by doing the truth, see John D. Caputo, *On Religion* (New York: Routledge, 2001), 28.

[11]See Miguel De La Torre, *Embracing Hopelessness* (Minneapolis: Fortress Press, 2017).

[12]James H. Cone, *The Cross and the Lynching Tree* (Maryknoll, NY: Orbis, 2011), 74–75, emphasis mine.

[13]Thomas G. Long, *The Witness of Preaching,* 3d ed. (Louisville: Westminster John Knox Press, 2016), 114–15, emphasis original.

[14]Kelly Brown Douglas, *Stand Your Ground: Black Bodies and the Justice of God* (Maryknoll, New York: Orbis Books, 2015), 225.

[15]For a more formal analysis of this structure, see Phil Snider, *Preaching after God: Derrida, Caputo, and the Language of Postmodern Homiletics* (Eugene, OR: Cascade,

2012), ch. 5. See also the afterword in this book, in which Rich Voelz names five additional characteristics of resistance preaching.

[16]I owe this insight to Elizabeth Grasham.

[17]Public Facebook post, December 10, 2017.

[18]I'm rewriting this section just one day after Emma Gonzalez's moving speech at a public rally against gun violence, and my mind keeps coming back to her words. The rally was held on February 17, 2018, just three days after the tragic shooting at Marjory Stoneman Douglas High School, where she was a senior at the time. She provides an example of profound, transformative public discourse. Listeners experience the longing for a better world, and are invited to go make it happen. See "Florida student Emma Gonzalez to lawmakers and gun advocates: 'We call BS,'" https://www.cnn.com/2018/02/17/us/florida-student-emma-gonzalez-speech/index.html. This is also part of the reason I included a reflection that was first published on Wil Gafney's blog; acts of public theology and biblical interpretation in the digital age provide wonderful opportunities for preachers to connect in ways otherwise not possible, and I want preachers to be mindful of them.

[19]Several of the sermons were edited from audio recordings and transcripts. Because sermons are generally written to be spoken instead of read, I've edited each of them for publication in book form.

[20]If one follows the trajectory of Christine Smith's homiletic, to which I'm deeply indebted, these sermons land within what she calls the third world of preaching, i.e. "the larger social context in which we live our lives of faith." Thus, they focus on "the particular issues, social systems, pervasive values, and theological understandings that dominate and structure the world in which we preach." She maintains that all three worlds are important for the preaching task. (The first world is the text; the second is the world of the preacher and their community, which includes emphases on spirituality, psychology, and social location.) See Smith, *Preaching as Weeping, Confession, and Resistance*, 1.

[21]For a brief introduction, see Carol Howard Merritt, "Liberty University, your roots are showing," The Christian Century, May 15, 2017, https://www.christiancentury.org/blog-post/liberty-university-your-roots-are-showing.

[22]See John D. Caputo, *The Weakness of God: A Theology of the Event* (Bloomington: Indiana University Press, 2006).

# Prologue

# When I Kept Silent

**Laura Jean Truman**

Laura Jean Truman is a queer writer, preacher, and former chaplain and pastor living in Atlanta, Georgia. She holds a BA in philosophy from the University of New Hampshire and an MDiv from Candler School of Theology. She supports her itinerant chaplaining, writing, and eternally optimistic church planting by slinging drinks at a historic bar in downtown Atlanta. This reflection was originally written on November 27, 2016, three Sundays after Donald Trump's electoral college victory.

• • •

*"Alas, Sovereign Lord," I said, "I do not know how to speak;
I am too young!"*

**Jeremiah 1:6 (NIV)**

I used to work as a chaplain at an elderly residential facility and rehab hospital in Atlanta. I was there on December 28, 2015, the day that the police officer who killed Tamir Rice was not indicted. I was scheduled to preach to a community of little old black ladies who marched in Alabama for civil rights, and little old white ladies who practiced racism as a daily ritual.

I haven't ever felt so young, ever, *ever*, as when I stood up to preach. I looked at all these people who leaned on me for spiritual care and guidance, and a fear/anger/sadness/anxiety ball sunk in my stomach, because *oh Jesus this little white girl from one of the whitest states in the U.S. who has only just barely graduated seminary is not prepared to do this.* Let's just skip this subject and preach something else, because what I was holding felt too heavy and too fragile for me to lift and not shatter.

I want to start by clarifying that this is not a story of me wildly succeeding as a White Savior to end racism in the course of a nine-minute sermon. And it's definitely not a story of me mastering how to talk about oppression when the oppressed and the oppressor are both in the room with me. It's not even a story about me owning my spiritual authority and leaning into my female empowerment as a pastor.

I'm not really sure what this story is about, but ever since the presidential election I can't stop thinking about all those elderly faces watching me, and how it felt to talk about evil when we all disagree about what evil is.

I started work at the nursing home in August of 2015, and by December, I was excelling at ducking and dodging all sensitive topics with my congregation. It was a politically and racially diverse hospital, which seemed like a really good reason to just talk about "Jesus Loves Me" all the time. I avoided taking a stand like it was my job (I may have actually told folks this was my job). I was Chaplain Laura Jean for the middle-aged Midwestern white man as well as the black trans woman on suicide watch. My work was to be present to every member of the community, to love well, to listen well, to hold them up in prayer, and when preaching, to preach the gospel of grace and the unfailing, unrelenting, unstoppable love of God through Jesus Christ.

I had underestimated a really central part of life in the nursing home. Everyone, of every political, religious, ethnic, racial identity, was watching the news. Nonstop. There isn't a whole lot to do in a nursing home except play bingo (not a stereotype! We loved bingo!), sing old Broadway musicals (my favorite unofficial chaplain position was Broadway pianist), and watch the news. Every time I knocked on a door and walked into someone's room, people talked about politics. People wanted to talk to the chaplain about the primaries and the next year's general election and about the immigrants and about the urban crime and police violence and the gay agenda and racist politicians. So I listened super well to everyone, and asked good questions, and worked hard to be present to every member of the community.

Every week, I got up and I preached on Monday and Tuesday and Wednesday to a racially mixed community about trusting God, faith in light of physical sickness, God as reconciler of relationships, Jesus as comforter to our loneliness, unrelenting grace for our own sins of resentment and fear and greed. And every week, in people's cramped, barren hospital rooms, I listened to the patter of anxiety while TVs ran in the background like a morbid soundtrack—prayers and reflections punctuated by CNN and an endless loop of gunshots and shaky cameras and black bodies dying in the road.

Then, the week after Christmas, a grand jury declined to indict the police officer who killed Tamir Rice, a 12-year-old black boy playing with a toy gun. The police officer pulled up in his car and shot him dead. The official record states it was less than two seconds after his arrival on the scene. The officer did not go to trial. Tamir was a little boy who likely hadn't even hit his growth spurt yet. He was still young enough that he probably wasn't embarrassed to be seen at the grocery store with his mom. We know that he liked to draw and play drums.

What I had started to feel somewhere in my gut was suddenly out loud and in my face. I had worked so hard to "be present to every member of the community" by avoiding difficult issues in public. That week I realized that my avoidance was also a statement—a statement of non-presence to my black residents. My silence said that both sides of the issue of racism had equal weight and that as a spiritual leader I was committed to letting evil hide as long as it was uncomfortable for me talk about. I had chosen the most vulnerable members of my congregation, and had decided that I'd address their fear and sorrow and anger privately, just in case I unsettled a cart of apples that I didn't have the skills to re-bag.

I had another sermon prepared that day and I threw it away. I sat in my car outside the building I worked in, and cried, and prayed, and looked at my watch because I had to walk into that building in 45 minutes to preach a sermon to my brokenhearted and oppressed and racist and lonely congregation.

There are times in a preacher's life when the lectionary is more than just a convenience, it's a sacred mandate. I went scrabbling to the lectionary to throw me a line and keep me from drowning, and the text for the week was Matthew 2:13–23. "The Slaughter of the Innocents."

> When Herod saw that he had been tricked by the wise men, he was infuriated, and he sent and killed all the children in and around Bethlehem who were two years old or under, according to the time that he had learned from the wise men. Then was fulfilled what had been spoken through the prophet Jeremiah: "A voice was heard in Ramah, wailing and loud lamentation, Rachel weeping for her children; she refused to be consoled, because they are no more." (Mt. 2:16–18)

Little boys, innocent children who didn't know the geopolitical scene they were born into, didn't know that they represented something terrifying and threatening to the powerful, didn't know that they weren't just "little children" but symbols of a deadly threat to the oppressor, little boys taken down in the streets by an insecure regime terrified of what they signified. Mothers weeping, because they didn't lose a symbol but their babies. Oppression driven by rage and above all, by fear. And always it's the babies, the innocent, the harmless, the different, the unarmed, that are shot down in the streets.

A voice is heard in Ramah, weeping and great mourning, Rachel weeping for her children and refusing to be comforted, because they are no more. The sorrow of black women and mothers and sisters, right here, in our sacred text.

I wrote my sermon on the back of a charting clipboard, and I don't have it anymore. What I remember most is how scared I was when I stood up. It would have been easier to preach to homogeny—to my seminarian friends, to the college ministry group, to the small liberal church plant. It was terrifying to preach to a room of beautiful ancient black women that I loved, that I was scared to betray by saying the wrong thing; and a room full of beautiful ancient white women who grew up in the South as far back as the 1920s and whose racism was rooted as deeply in their hearts as their identity—and who I also loved, loved, loved so much.

What I preached that day was probably 80 percent wrong, unhelpful, overly self-righteous, or overly capitulating. I "spoke of things that I did not understand" and spoke to people that I barely understood.

But I did speak. Too late, too young, too wrong, too complex, overly simplified—but none of those things were silence.

Scripture gives us a lot of ways to speak. It's rich with language for calling angry judgment on pastors and priests (Malachi), mocking authorities with potty humor (Elijah: "LOL, maybe your God is on the toilet hehe"), for performance art as activism (Jeremiah), for calling rulers to repentance with metaphors (Nathan), for answering questions in the dead of night with the religious leaders (Jesus), and also for calling religious leaders names (also Jesus). The only thing that is not a powerful force against injustice in scripture is silence.

The only thing that is not a powerful force against injustice in scripture is silence.

I'm going to get it wrong. You're also going to get it wrong. I've already gotten it wrong a ridiculous amount of times and I'm not even to my 30s yet. Some days I'll be too gentle toward evil, and some days I'll be too self-righteous toward humans made in the image of God. I'm going to be angry when I should be listening well, and listen silently when I should be angry at injustice. I'm going to get called out, sometimes kindly and sometimes angrily, by people that I hurt when I get it wrong. And I'm going to have to learn how to humbly course-correct myself when I'm called out, so that I keep learning how to speak, when to speak, and what to say.

These are weird and confusing and evil times. Don't let fear of getting it wrong keep you from saying what your conscience prods you to say. Listen humbly, be kind, be angry, and speak bravely.

# 1

# Beloved Resistance
# (Or, the Sunday after Tuesday)

**Molly Housh Gordon**

Rev. Molly Housh Gordon is the minister of Unitarian Universalist Church in Columbia, Missouri. She's a graduate of Hendrix College and Harvard Divinity School. This sermon was preached to her congregation on November 13, 2016—the first Sunday after the general election.

• • •

*1 John 4:7*

My dear UU Churchers. My beloved community. I love you, and I know many of you are hurting right now.

You might be hurting because the oppression that you've experienced all your life has fueled a presidential campaign and has now seemingly been given the legitimacy of the highest office in the land by millions of voters. The pain of racism toward people of color, Islamophobia toward Muslims, xenophobia toward immigrants, homophobia and transphobia toward LGBTQ+ individuals, ableism toward people with disabilities, misogyny toward women—this pain is amplified by 59.4 million votes explicitly or implicitly supporting such hate-filled words and deeds. It hurts.

Or you might be hurting because you carry the wounds of sexual assault, and an unrepentant sexual predator has been elected to the office of president.

You might be hurting because you fear your rights, your marriage, or your family are at risk in a homophobic administration.

You might be hurting because you fear the health care you can afford for yourself and your family will be revoked, your own well-being repealed and replaced with God knows what.

You might be hurting because you fear or have experienced physical or emotional violence at the hands of people who feel they have been given permission to act out their hatred, and who have already committed more than two hundred acts of directly related harassment or violence since Tuesday.

Or you might be hurting because you are deeply afraid for loved ones whose lives or livelihood feel at risk in this climate of division.

Beloveds in this room, beloveds in Columbia, and beloveds beyond. We see your pain and fear. We know it is real. We know it matters. Your pain matters. Your whole heart matters, because it will take a whole lot of fierce, busted up, beating hearts to counteract this hate.

So we've got to do what we can to stay wholehearted.

A commentator named Sarah Fields wrote this week: "Hate is a bodyguard for grief. When people lose the hate, they are forced to deal with the pain beneath."[1] The corollary is true: When we don't deal with our pain and anger and fear, they harden into hate, they deepen into despair, they freeze into cynical isolation.

When we numb our hard feelings and fail to speak them, we let them fester and grow, rather than using their purifying fire to fuel our living and loving. Fear and pain festering is what got us into this mess, and so we must bring ours, now, into the light of day and the power of community. Today we roust the monster out from under the bed—to be overcome by our courageous love.

On Tuesday night, when the cynical triumph of anxiety and division became clear, I was distressed by my own first response, which was isolation. I looked at my sleeping baby and my worried spouse, and I thought, "Okay, time to batten down the hatches." Everyone else be damned, I will take care of my own and we will survive.

Maybe some of you felt, or feel, the same way. Maybe you've joked about moving away, or considered it seriously. The natural impulse in times of intensity and fear is often run away, numb it out, close our hearts, clench them like a fist. It is human to feel that way.

But our faith is in doors thrown wide and hands outstretched and hearts improbably and courageously open to connection because connection is what will save us. I could build a wall around my heart, but guess who would pay for that wall? My very soul. My deepest, human-most soul, which depends desperately for its survival on the survival and connection of every other soul.

So I followed a friend's advice, to work on keeping my heart open with the help of my breath and a few choice and raging words: I spoke aloud of my fears to my spouse. I wept for the world my daughter and every other baby child will inherit. I reached out to others who were afraid. I read the courageous and galvanizing words and experiences of those most marginalized by these forces of hatred.

Then I followed my mom's advice and went to sleep.

I awoke on Wednesday morning in grief. But I also awoke as though layers of inhibition and distraction and willful ignorance and fear to act had burned away in the purifying fire of that grief. I awoke with a clarity I have never known, about the work of my life, and the work of the church in this time of renewed and legitimized oppression and division.

I awoke less afraid of what people will think of me if I truly live out the absurd and vulnerable calling of love—because we are vulnerable anyway, and the absurdity of love may be the only thing that saves us.

I woke up less reserved about my expressions of connection. I found myself telling people I never tell that I love them. Because I do, and how can we not add more affection to this world, right?

And I woke up with a clarity and renewed commitment to our community. Never have I been more sure of the mission of our church and of our Unitarian Universalist faith—to nourish and sustain wholeness of heart, and to humbly join our hearts to the resistance.

To become relentless, uninhibited, wild, and wise with our love.

Anything that gets in the way of whole hearts joining a movement of liberation and connection, anything that gets in the way has got to go. There is too much at stake for us to be distracted.

Nothing can stand in the way between our love and the world. And I don't mean this in a fuzzy, sticky, can't we all just get along kind of way. I mean this in the knowledge that Love transforms us, even those hardest of heart. I mean this in the knowledge that hatred is the hell that exists only in the human heart, and that it is our deepest work to Love the Hell out of this world.

We must love at the margins, we must love at the intersections, and we must eventually love in the centers of power. In the end, it will be only love with the power to win the hearts of those now swallowed by fear and division. But for this moment our priority is clear. Our first priority must be love at the margins—a strong, embodied, risky presence with those who are already at risk, most vulnerable to the hatred of this time.

Maybe you and your family would like to start with a project that my colleague Ashley Horan originated on Wednesday that she's calling neighborhood love notes: using sidewalk chalk to create messages of solidarity with those now more vulnerable to hatred. Messages like: Love wins. Black Lives Matter. Peace to our Muslim siblings. You belong. We love you. You are welcome. There is chalk here for you to take with you if you'd like to find a place to create some Love Notes today or this week.

Of course, this is just a start, an art, a symbol of a larger commitment to presence and solidarity that we must now figure out how to live into, together. I want you to know that I am committed, and our mission of radical welcome, deep connection, and healing the world shows that we as a community are committed to be one of the places where we do that work of solidarity and love.

We will be and we will become a community of resistance and hope.

But here's one important understanding we must recall about this presence to and with those now most vulnerable. No matter who you are, but especially if you are male, and especially if you are cisgender, and especially if you are heterosexual, and especially if you are white: we must recall that it is not ours to save others like a shining white knight.

The truth is, rather, that presence with marginalized people, deep connections of solidarity—and an ever greater capacity to show up with humility and love—is what will save us. It will save us.

White people particularly, and people from dominant groups generally, need to be clear in our understanding that none of this hatred or oppression is new. It has been alive and well and active in our country, no matter who has been president.

It's just so blatant, so dangerously legitimized, so vaunted in this moment that many white folks are waking up further or waking up for the first time to the depths of a reality of racism, xenophobia, misogyny, and more, from which some level of privilege has shielded us.

As one commentator put it, the wolf in sheep's clothing is now simply the wolf in wolf's clothing. Of course this is not to say that things aren't legitimately more dangerous for those continually marginalized by our society—put the wolf in the highest office in the land and you can expect some to be hunted.

But perhaps it is to say that vulnerable communities in our country are not shocked at the level of vitriol and hate, and they are not unprepared to resist it. On the contrary, marginalized communities will rightly be our most potent source of wisdom, know-how, clarity, and leadership in our day.

In such a time as this, we must cast our lot with those who resist—indeed, with those who've always resisted. We must learn at their feet. From the many histories of movement for human liberation, in our faith traditions, across the world: from the civil rights leaders who are still with us as elders and sages; from trans folks and people with disabilities and others who know what it is to claim a dignity denied by culture; from the queer women of color and others building a movement for black lives; from Native leaders protecting our water, the latest in generations of struggle. In such a time as this, we must join the movement for the sake of our souls. We must follow the lead of those who resist, because theirs is the work of deeper connection and more demanding love.

As blogger Courtney Parker West writes: "People of color have always resisted and you can follow us. You can't be with her anymore, so be with us."[2]

Or in the words of the African American blogger and cultural commentator Jay Smooth, who released a videoblog on Tuesday night saying this to his communities of color: "I don't know that we will survive. I don't know that we will be okay. But what I know is that we will resist. We come from a tradition of resistance . . ." He continues: "They wanna talk about 'Make America Great Again.' What I know is the only glimpse of greatness this country has ever had, the only glimpse of the ideals this country was founded on that we've ever had is because of our resistance."[3]

In a time such as this, we cast our lot with those who resist, with those who have always resisted. We join the movement as though our lives depend on it, because they do. Because our souls are saved by the movement of hearts made whole and connected with love.

My dear UU Churchers, the forces of fear in this world are powerful. We knew that. But more powerful is the courage of those who resist, who have always resisted. More powerful is the calling Love places upon our lives—we know this too.

Never has that calling been more clear.

---

[1] As quoted by Charles Eisenstein in "The Election: Of Hate, Grief, and a New Story," November 10, 2016, https://charleseisenstein.net/essays/hategriefandanewstory/.

[2] Courtney Parker West, "A guide for 'shocked' white friends who want to help people of color after the election," Quartz, November 15, 2016, https://qz.com/836930/election-2016-a-guide-for-white-friends-who-want-to-help-people-of-color/.

[3] Jay Smooth, "Trump's America: This Is What Happens Now," *YouTube*, November 9, 2016, https://www.youtube.com/watch?time_continue=3&v=MqMhx6vh0VY.

# 2

# When to Break the Law

**Erin Wathen**

Rev. Erin Wathen is the senior minister of St. Andrew Christian Church (Disciples of Christ) in Olathe, Kansas. She is the author of *Resist and Persist: Faith and the Fight for Equality* and *More Than Words: 10 Values for the Modern Family.* This sermon was preached at St. Andrew Christian Church on January 29, 2017.

• • •

## Luke 6:1–11

On *The Moth* radio hour last week, Greg Audel shared his story.[1] He talked about a childhood in a home with no rules. His parents were, as he said, "Busy with their own things," and didn't place many expectations on his habits or behavior. He slept when he wanted, ate what he wanted, and went to school when he felt like it. Which wasn't often.

But then when he was 12 years old, something shifted. He started going to a private school that was about 30 miles from his house, and there he made good friends with another boy who lived much closer to the school. He started spending time at this friend's house. Audel says the first time he went home with his friend, they had after-school snacks. Well, that's quaint, he thought.

And the first time he heard the dad ask to see his son's homework, Audel said to his friend, "Are you going to take that from him?"

But then, his friend's mother told them it was time to get ready for bed. And Audel teared up . . . Never in life had anyone told him to go to bed.

He then went into the bathroom . . . where a toothbrush had been laid out for him. The mom stuck her head in and said, "If you want to throw your clothes in the hamper, I'll be happy to wash them for you." So that by the time they got to bed, he was literally sobbing . . . because he had never experienced these particular expressions of love and care before. It was a whole new world as he began to see that "rules, routines and structure... had value."

So, you heard it here first, kids. Bedtime, homework, and curfew . . . that is a love language.

What's interesting is that the title of this segment has nothing to do with rules, or discipline. Instead, it's called "Finding My Village." It goes to show how powerfully a few simple rules can shape a sense of belonging . . . how sharing expectations and boundaries is a big part of what forges a family connection.

"My friend's parents said that I could stay there anytime I wanted," he said. "So I pretty much stayed for the next 5 years."

Some of the rules that we live by, as civilized people, are for our own good. There are traffic laws, laws against stealing, laws against doing bodily harm to another person. And some of the rules that order our lives are more of a covenantal nature . . . things that bind us as family and community, but are not legally binding.

In Jesus's world, Sabbath law was both: a law and a covenant. A central part of community and family life, Sabbath law was meant to restore the body, connect the family, and even serve justice by providing a needed break for workers, and even the land itself.

Which is why the Sabbath law was the perfect issue for the Pharisees to leverage when they wanted to back Jesus into a corner. It was a great hot-button ideological issue that touched every part of life. That's why we frequently come upon stories in scripture like this one, otherwise known as the "Sabbath controversies." If the authorities can catch Jesus doing something on the Sabbath day that counts as work, they can easily say, "Look, he clearly doesn't know how we do things."

Jesus healing on the Sabbath day, or looking the other way as the disciples grind some grain for their breakfast, creates the perfect opportunity, and the Pharisees are ready. "See?" they say to the onlookers. "He doesn't know the rules. He isn't one of us."

As always, however, Jesus does not submit to their legalistic pop quiz. Instead, he changes the conversation. He shifts the focus from the letter of the law (which, obviously, he knows as well as they do) to the spirit of the law. And that, as we know, is when things always get interesting with Jesus.

Because the spirit of the law is far more complex than its wording. In this case, Jesus says, the spirit of the law is not about what day it is, or what counts as work and what doesn't. It's about right and wrong; it's about doing good vs. doing what is evil. No matter what the law says, the word on the page is never more important than the person in front of you. When someone is hungry, you feed them. When someone is injured, you heal what's hurting. Laws have their place in our lives, but ultimately, you have to be in the moment, and root your actions in love. You have to ask if keeping the law, in this moment, will give life—or take it away.

This is a moment of empowerment that Jesus gives to his disciples, to the onlookers, and to all who would come and hear this word later. It is a call to live, not just within the law, but within the deeper covenants that bind us as people of God. It is a call to the hard work of discernment; to not rely on written rules to guide our conscience; but to dig deeper. To find that intersection of our humanity and the Holy Spirit, recognizing that no legitimate law calls us to let another person suffer. And if it does, then that law goes against the deeper covenant of who we are.

So, for instance—just hypothetically speaking, of course—if you were a national park ranger, and a word comes forth that says you can no longer share information with the public about the environment, or climate change . . . Well, then that law goes against your deepest values; your beliefs about stewardship of the earth, and the shared ownership of our greatest national treasures. So maybe you have to go rogue. Maybe you create an "Alt" Twitter account, so that you can still engage the public, and share actual facts. Maybe you even inspire a growing resistance . . . so that within 24 hours there is also an AltNASA Twitter account, an AltUSForestService, and an UngaggedEPA; all positioned to voice opposition to the growing threat against the environment.

Or maybe you are the mayor of a sanctuary city. And maybe your government threatens to come in and do broad deportation sweeps. That goes against every expectation you and your community have established about what it means to be a place of welcome and inclusion. So maybe you stand at a lectern, with cameras flashing, surrounded by your people . . . and maybe you look into those cameras, lean into those microphones and you say, "not in our house. This is not who we are."[2]

Maybe your name is Mark Hetfield, and you are the president of HIAS— one of the largest refugee resettlement organizations in the country. And the powers that be say that refugees aren't welcome here anymore. That's when you make a public statement and say "Faith groups are going to kick and scream and object to every aspect of this vile executive order that makes America something it is not." Maybe you say something like that.[3]

And if you are a person deeply committed to interfaith relationships, and your president passes a thinly veiled maneuver to keep Muslims out of your country . . . then maybe you send the ACLU to every airport in America and watch this bill get lawyered to death. You stand up and you say "that law has no life in it. This is not who we are."[4]

Because, after all, we have been shaped by the things that bind us. Rules and customs; shared values and expectations; the law of the land and the covenants of community. We value all of these things too deeply to let any of them be distorted; manipulated by those hungry for power or filled with hate. We do not let that stand, because we know who we are. We know who we are together, and we know who we are in Christ.

Jesus calls us to live by a higher calling than the word on the page, the letter of the law. We are called to live by the rule of heart, the inner voice of the holy. We are led to that sacred intersection of our humanity and the

Holy Spirit, and when we find that place, we are empowered to discern what is right in the moment; and to meet the need in front of us.

Of course, there is a difference between laws that are legally binding, and those of our covenantal relationships. There is a time and place for both, and all of these boundaries serve to shape us in some way. But ultimately, it is not the letter of the law that shapes us . . . it is the spirit of love and transformation that we have known in Christ and community; it is this higher calling to be people who heal, and feed, and show mercy. And when, from time to time, the law of the land is at odds with who we are as people of faith—then we push the edges of the law, as Jesus did.

We may not always know when it's time to do that. But Jesus gave us a simple test to know what is right, in any given moment. We just have to ask ourselves a few simple questions. Is it good? Is it just? Does it protect the vulnerable, or give more authority to the powerful?

Does the law give life, or take it away?

Sometimes rule breaking is a love language of its own.

---

[1]See Greg Audel, "Finding My Village," *The Moth: True Stories Told Live*, January 17, 2017, https://themoth.org/stories/finding-my-village.

[2]See Liz Robbins, "'Sanctuary City' Mayors Vow to Defy Trump's Immigration Order," *The New York Times*, January 25, 2017, https://www.nytimes.com/2017/01/25/nyregion/outraged-mayors-vow-to-defy-trumps-immigration-order.html?_r=0.

[3]See Tom Gjelten, "Trump Refugee Ban Clashes with Faith-Based Groups' Religious Missions," *National Public Radio*, January 27, 2017, https://www.npr.org/2017/01/27/511997346/trump-refugee-ban-clashes-with-faith-based-groups-religious-missions.

[4]See Ben Dreyfuss, "A Federal Judge Just Issued a Stay against Donald Trump's 'Muslim Ban,'" *Mother Jones*, January 29, 2017, https://www.motherjones.com/politics/2017/01/muslim-ban-federal-court/.

# 3

# Answering the Call to Prayer

**Alton B. Pollard III**

Rev. Dr. Alton B. Pollard III is president of Louisville Presbyterian Theological Seminary. He is an ordained Baptist minister and the author of many books and articles, including *Mysticism and Social Change*. A version of this sermon was preached as part of the Installation Week of Services for Rev. Dr. Darryl D. Roberts, new pastor of Nineteenth Street Baptist Church in Washington, D.C., on February 16, 2017.

• • •

### Matthew 6:9–13; Luke 11:1–4

Few things in life bring more joy than spending time with loved ones, family, and friends. We were grateful to have our children at home with us for the Christmas holidays. One afternoon my daughter and I decided to watch a movie. Many of you may be familiar with *The Siege*, a 1998 political thriller starring Denzel Washington. It remains to this day a controversial film about U.S. patriotism gone wrong and terrorism on American soil in response; it features fearmongering against Muslim Americans and national innocence lost. Religious and ethnic bigotry, much like racism, is as American as apple pie.

My daughter and I talked about the imposition of martial law in the film, whether it's possible in America today, and the implications for our democracy were it to occur. We solemnly remembered the enslavement of Africa's progeny on these shores, the near extermination, removal, and relocation of this land's indigenous peoples, and the forced internment of Japanese Americans during the 1940s. We discussed the growing library of Hollywood cinema that describes an undesirable future that seems all too real: *1984*, *A Clockwork Orange*, *Blade Runner*, *Soylent Green*, *Children of Men*, *V for Vendetta*, *The Book of Eli*, *I Am Legend*, *The Mad Max* series, *The Matrix* series, and *The Handmaid's Tale*, among others. We talked about the current crop of movies that capitalize on the apprehensions of youth and young adults: *The Hunger Games* series, the *Insurgent* series, *The Maze Runner* series, *The Giver, Ender's Game,* and *The 5th Wave,* to name a few.

Some of these films border on the fantastic or the surreal. Others seem like they're on the verge of happening now. "Utopia" is the word we frequently invoke to describe a society that knows no conflict, hunger, hierarchy, or unhappiness. It's the future that much of humanity truly longs for, a perfect paradise, idyllic, joyous, and free. It's the biblical garden of Eden, Buddhism's Nirvana, Hinduism's Moksha, Dr. Martin Luther King Jr.'s Beloved Community, and Bishop Desmond Tutu's Rainbow Children. It's the good society, with world peace; the very Commonwealth of God.

"Dystopia" presents quite the opposite view of the future and our world. Society is filled with hopelessness, division, misery, pain, and strife. Whether the cause is due to some environmental disaster, dwindling natural resources, political dictatorship, or military or alien intervention, dystopian life is described as gray, bleak, undesirable, oppressive, and absolutely horrifying. The decay of civil society, willful disregard for civic decency, suppression of dissent, rampant inequality, numbing anonymity and the loss of freedoms are its result. Dystopia is what happens to a people, any people, when a society's dreams turn to nightmares. Totalitarian regimes, the fascist state, autocratic rule, dictatorship . . . it goes by many names.

Does any of this sound at all familiar? Some would say dystopia is fast becoming our reality now. I will let you be the judge.

It's the month in which we formally celebrate black history. But it's my experience to celebrate black history each and every day of the year. Black history is a time to look back on our ancestral past and look forward with anticipation to our bright future as a people. We remember and never forget how we have come, "over a way that with tears has been watered."[1] We give God thanks in the words of the old hymns "for how we got ovah" and "how we overcome." We pay homage to our foremothers and forefathers. We give honor to the elders, those sturdy oaks and living libraries among us. We celebrate the glad task of raising our children and young people well. We rejoice in our community's complex and incredible heritage. We embrace our sacred call. In loving ourselves deeply, we prepare for the challenges of tomorrow today.

It really does not need to be said that overt racial and ethnic tensions and all manner of social unrest have returned with a vengeance in our own day and time. Indeed, a new crisis emerges virtually every day. Equally tragic, too many of our churches are still yet searching for a way to be relevant in the midst of empire, not knowing we don't have to look far at all to practice our faith. Everywhere we look out on the streets, in our neighborhoods, in our own homes, in the workplace, on our way to church Sunday morning, there are young people who have never been to church. They don't know the meaning of the church. What they do know is the church does not care for them. The church is not there for them. To paraphrase brother theologian James Baldwin, "nobody knows their name."[2] Yes, "[t]he harvest is plentiful, but the laborers are few" (Mt. 9:37).

People everywhere of all faiths—including persons of ambivalent faith and those who profess no faith at all—are in search of deep sustenance. They're seeking meaning and resources to renew their strength at just the time when many of us had hoped the struggles for social justice and our communal liberation in the 20th century were almost won. However, not only have last century urgencies returned with a vengeance, they're compounded and magnified by a growing sense of alienation throughout society and a lack of personal fulfillment in this century.

People don't always know what they're looking for; they only know they don't want what they see. They're looking for a beacon, a witness, anything, a sign. They're searching for some form of reassurance that there really is more to life than this, that goodness has the last word in life. Something has gone terribly wrong in our world. We simply seem to have gone off the rails. Our moral compass is broken and our collective destiny as a nation hurtles toward self-destruction. In the midst of the American madness, the struggle for our common humanity continues anew.

Many of us who are believers have grown weary and are defeated in the face of our present dangers. In the wake of our most recent presidential elections and a hostile social and political climate, we don't want to hear about the news, turn on the news, read the news, or discuss the news that comes from any form of media, whether the news source is liberal, conservative, tabloid, or "fake." Even in our congregations the "good news" we preach about Jesus, Mary's brown baby and Joseph's son, seems to be in short supply.

As African Americans, our every ambition to wipe out long centuries of oppression in a very short while has taken its heavy toll. Every success we've made is seeded with just enough distress, doubt, and destruction to at times deflate our proud and right sense of accomplishment. Every personal victory seems tainted because we sometimes falter. Yes, we sometimes stumble and fall.

We remember with fierce pride the determination of our ancestors to make it through every danger, toil, and snare. Our souls look back and wonder, What about us? Do we have the same courage? Do we have what it takes? For every step forward we seem to take one step back. For every door opened another door seems to close. We know that we have made significant personal and social gains. We know that as a community we are in some ways better. Yet still, our cumulative attainments and personal achievements have not led to the whole survival of our people.

The pain is so deep and the longing is so intense. Our lives are in distress and we yearn for perfect peace. We aspire to more in this mortal frame. Often, what we feel cannot be assuaged by our conventional creeds or confessions; is not appeased by our customary turns to worship or liturgy, testimony or praise. Our hearts cry out. Our souls are hungry. Our spirits thirst. Just beneath the surface of our carefully orchestrated and postmodern forms of black worship, just beneath our now trendy claims to be "spiritual but not religious," our Creator calls. God is the air we breathe. God is the song we sing. God is our inward journey. God is our upward reach. God is our source and our supply. God is the joy and strength of our lives. God is the one whom we absolutely and positively cannot live without.

In prayer we gather up the broken pieces, retrieve that which we have lost, and move toward the One who sustains us every waking moment of our lives. In prayer we lay our all on the altar. In prayer we aspire to the practice of Presence. In prayer we enter into the experience of holiness. In prayer we're searched and known. In prayer we're met at our deepest need. In prayer we find the antidote to empire and its minions. In prayer we meet joy, unspeakable joy! This morning we're answering the call for human wholeness, justice and life, standing in the need of prayer.

My soul says "Yes" when Howard Thurman, African American griot and mystic exemplar of the faith, writes, "I am always impressed by the fact that it's recorded that the only thing that the disciples asked Jesus to teach them how to do was to pray."[3]

We know that Jesus's own dependence on prayer was active and constant; he lived to worship, to be at one with God:

> In the morning, while it was still very dark, he got up and went out to a deserted place, and there he prayed. (Mark 1:35)

> After saying farewell to them, he went up on the mountain to pray. (Mark 6:46)

> [M]any crowds would gather to hear him and to be cured of their diseases. But he would withdraw to deserted places and pray. (Luke 5:15–16)

> Now during those days he went out to the mountain to pray; and he spent the night in prayer to God. (Luke 6:12)

> He was praying in a certain place, and after he had finished, one of his disciples said to him, "Lord, teach us to pray, as John taught his disciples." (Luke 11:1)

Like the disciples, we too want to know the power of prayer as our own. I don't know about you, but I want to hear God calling me. A great while before the day, at the close of the day, in the stillness of the night, in the light of the day, at noontime, in the midnight hour, in the hunger of my own heart, in the depths of my spirit, in the struggles of my life, in my time of grief, in my seasons of success. On this day, in this time, right here, right now. I need Emmanuel, God with me.

Day after day, we see the human condition in all its ugliness and messiness, and often far more than we see its beauty and worth. The killing of black lives. The profiling of the young. The violence against women. The stigmatization of LGBTQ+ persons. The disregard for the poor. The discrimination against immigrants. The banning of Muslims. The defilement of Native burial grounds. The contempt for universal health care. The destruction of public school education. The bullying of children and teens. The defiling of houses of worship. The desecration of religious faiths. The disrespect of persons. The resurgence of xenophobia. The rejection of science. The war against safe drinking water. The denial of climate change. The rising tide of hate groups. The domestic extremists. The homegrown terrorists. The mass murders. The serial murders. The very destruction of our planet earth. Many of us have sought common cause against the hatred, the meanness, the division, and the death for so long, on our own terms, in our own way that maybe and at last we are finally ready to try God. Across our many religious traditions and social circumstances it's time to answer the empowering call to prayer.

We gather this morning in quietness and confidence, in prayer and supplication, with petitions and praise, with testimonies and songs of thanksgiving, in the spirit of Christian unity and solidarity, lifting our voices to the one and only wise God. Your pastor prays. You are a praying congregation. It's a match made in heaven when pastor and people hunger and thirst for righteousness, are drum majors for justice, and prayer warriors for peace. It's altogether beautiful when we seek God's face together.

For such a time as this, we need the power of prayer. Church, pray when you are at your most phenomenal. Pray when you believe you are at your most fallible. Pray when, like Langston Hughes, you "have seen rivers" and "life ain't been no crystal stair."[4] Pray when you are in your secret closet. Pray when you are feeling vulnerable. Pray, in the spirit of Toni Morrison, when you are alone "with your own best self."[5] Pray together, where two or three are gathered (Mt. 18:20). Pray because the whole world stands in desperate need.

Prayer changes things. Prayer changes the one who prays. Prayer changes the pray-er. You become part of the answer. Prayer gives you clear vision. Prayer is a call to consciousness. Prayer clothes us in our right mind. Prayer gives us courage. Prayer calls us to transgress. Prayer calls us to do justice. Prayer calls us to organize, strategize, and effect change. Prayer calls us to be agents for transformation. Through prayer we become the change we seek. As my former pastor used to say, "No prayer, no power. Little prayer, little power. Much prayer, much power." Pray in and out of season. Pray without ceasing. Pray my strength and I will pray yours.

My prayer for you and me is not to accept the things we cannot change, but to have the courage to change the things we cannot accept. We will succeed, because God wants us to succeed, for the sake of God's world.[6]

---

[1]From James Weldon Johnson's hymn, "Lift Every Voice and Sing," commonly referred to as the Black National Anthem.

[2]See James Baldwin, *Nobody Knows My Name* (New York: Vintage; Reissue, 1992).

[3]Howard Thurman, *Disciplines of the Spirit* (Richmond, IN: Friends United Press, 1963), 88–89.

[4]Excerpted from "The Negro Speaks of Rivers" and "Mother to Son." See Langston Hughes and Arnold Rampersad, ed., *The Collected Poems of Langston Hughes* (New York: Vintage, 1995).

[5]Paraphrasing Paul D's concluding words to Sethe: "You your own best thing, Sethe. You are." Toni Morrison, *Beloved* (New York: Alfred A. Knopf, 1987), 273.

[6]Editor's note: this sermon concluded with the poem "and when the revelation came," by Carolyn Rodgers. While copyright laws prevent us from publishing the poem here, it's available in Carolyn M. Rodgers, *how i got ovah: New and Selected Poems* (Garden City, NY: Anchor Press/Doubleday, 1976), 65–67.

# 4

# Everything Must Change

**Amy Butler**

Rev. Dr. Amy Butler is the senior minister of the historic Riverside Church in the City of New York. She holds degrees from Baylor University, the International Baptist Theological Seminary, and Wesley Theological Seminary. Her work has been featured in numerous outlets, including *The Washington Post, The New York Times, The Wall Street Journal, National Public Radio,* and *USA Today.* This Palm Sunday sermon was preached at the Riverside Church on March 19, 2017.

• • •

### Matthew 21:1–11

Try to imagine what it was like that day. The weather hadn't started to get oppressively hot in the desert yet; the air was still cool, especially at night. And up there on the Mount of Olives, a long ridge running beside Jerusalem and looking over into the city, there was a breeze that rustled their cloaks and felt a little bit like optimism. I imagine it must have been sunny that day, too. But it wasn't just the weather. As they looked out over the city they could see that it was turned out in all its finery, the white marble and gold trim of the temple shining in the sun. Entering the gates from every side of the city the traffic was constant, so many people arriving to visit family or to worship at the temple during Passover, some of the holiest days of the Jewish year.

Jesus himself had been, for some weeks, making his way toward Jerusalem. He'd been in the countryside preaching and healing people, picking up new followers who heard his message of love and justice and wondered if he would be the one who would finally deliver the Jewish people from Roman oppression.

Now Jesus stood, looking out over Jerusalem, a city he loved. Perhaps he glanced over his shoulder at the crowd who'd followed him this far. He knew that this was a defining moment: that they were headed toward a collision, a crash between oppressive powers of religion and government, and his gospel of love and justice. Whatever was ahead, it would require such commitment and clarity, an understanding of faith as something we live out loud. Maybe the people standing with Jesus knew what was ahead; maybe they didn't. But as he stood there looking out over the city, · Jesus certainly knew this: *we don't really start living until we find out what we'll die for.*

Today is Palm Sunday, and as we stand on the edge of Holy Week we are still thinking about the work of Lent, how God perpetually invites us to change, to rethink the way we live, to step out from our human constructs of life and into a world that God dreams for us.

But change is difficult, and the world is dangerous, and we are scared.

And this is precisely why we call this the work of Lent—it's hard. Trying to imagine a different way of living, trying to step into that new way. It will take everything we have: our deepest commitment, our truest resolve, our utmost dedication.

Matthew's gospel today tells the story of a small crowd waving palms on the edge of Jerusalem, and it presents an invitation to us to change the way in which we understand the expression of our faith. So many of us have learned that a life of faith is the exercise of following an inviolable list of rules, our successful following of which will get us into heaven, and our failure to follow, well, you know.

But I wonder as we set out into this holiest of weeks, whether we're being invited to understand our faith less as following rules and more as speaking up, as being mouthpieces for righteousness, insisting on justice and peace and wholeness for all of humanity.

God's way in this world, after all, runs directly counter to systems of oppression and exploitative power. It seems to me, then, that our view of faith must change. Everything about it must change: from an understanding of faith as compliance to an understanding of faith as protest. Speaking up. Refusing to be silent. Not getting tired. Risking everything.

After all, this week especially, Holy Week, if we didn't know it before, we certainly will by Friday: *we don't even begin living . . . until we find out what we'll die for.*

All four gospel accounts tell some version of this story, which takes place, remember, just before the start of Passover. Recall that Passover is a holy time of remembrance for Jews then, even as it is now. Passover lasts for eight days and is the marking of the hardship of oppression in Egypt, the calling of Moses to lead the people to freedom, to a Promised Land flowing with milk and honey, the hurried preparations to be ready to flee, the miraculous parting of the Red Sea, the hardship of 40 years wandering in the desert, the giving of the Ten Commandments. In the marking of that miraculous history, Passover asks the question: Now that we are free, how shall we live? What does the Lord require of us?

To remember. To remember that the journey from oppression to freedom, from unjust violence to just nonviolence, has not been completed. Jews then and now leave the door open, leave an empty seat for Elijah, and tell the story in first person—as if they were there—so that one day, finally, with our participation, the will of God will be done on earth as it is in heaven.

It sounds a bit like discontent: pushing back against unjust systems; being unwilling to sit silent while oppression continues; insisting on the way of God in a world that does not recognize it; protest.

Filled with travelers and tourists that day, we should also remember that Jerusalem was under the punishing rule of the Roman Empire, its people oppressed and living with the crippling burden of high taxes and limited agency. The crowds were thick and keeping the peace was the number one priority of Roman governor Pontius Pilate and his troops. He wanted to make sure that the people didn't get too riled up in their Passover celebration. And, he wanted to be sure they remembered who was in charge.

In fact, as part of the festivities of the week and in an effort to show Roman dominance, Pilate had planned a procession into Jerusalem led by Pilate himself. No one in the city could miss it: a huge display with Pilate prancing in on a war horse and legions of Roman soldiers with their gleaming armor marching in concert. They entered through the western gate, the big main gate that framed a bustling thoroughfare.

People lined the streets waving and cheering, families staked out places on the parade route just so they could watch the army make its way in. It would have been like a celebrity sighting—people craned to get a glimpse of the powerful regent who ruled the whole area where the city of Jerusalem was located.

The message of Pilate and the Roman emperor was clear: it may be the Feast of the Passover, but this holiday was only being celebrated at the pleasure of the Roman rulers. And no Jew living in Jerusalem or visiting the city for Passover should dare to think of this as anything other than a nice little religious celebration, generously allowed by the magnanimous and gracious permission of the Roman government.

As Jesus stood on the Mount of Olives looking out over Jerusalem, he could see right out in front of him the road to the city, winding steeply down past groves of olive trees, into the deep Kidron Valley, and then sharply back uphill into Jerusalem through the east side, a smaller gate in the back of the city. And we should know that the crowd gathered to cheer Jesus was miniscule in comparison to the huge group watching Pilate's parade on the other side of the city.

Pilate rode in through the main gate; Jesus rode in through a small gate in the back of the city. Pilate was dressed in his finery, riding a huge warhorse; Jesus had no armor with no Roman insignia . . . and his ride was the colt of a donkey. The people at the front gate pledged their loyalty to the Roman government and cheered the military might they saw. The little crowd at the back gate, led by children waving palms, yelled "Hosanna!"—roughly translated "Lord, help us"—and followed it with the treasonous, "Blessed is the one who comes in the name of the Lord!" (Mt. 21:9) Everything about Jesus's entry was a protest to the big parade going on right across town.

Once we see the true setting of this story of Jesus on a little donkey and people waving palms and shouting, we can see very clearly that everything must change; that our understanding of faith must be always grounded in protest.

You may have learned in Sunday school that everyone in Jerusalem got it that day. That's what I learned, anyway . . . that for that one glorious moment all the people understood who Jesus was and vowed to follow him, joining their voices and their lives to speak up for God's way of love in the world.

It wasn't so. It's never been that easy to follow Jesus, even on Palm Sunday.

No, anyone in Jerusalem that day who managed to get through the crowds pressing in around Pilate on the other side of town, just to get to the back gate in time to see Jesus led in the back gate on a little donkey, knew—they knew for sure that what they were seeing was not a popular endorsement of God's kingdom coming to be, but a visual demonstration of how much God's way of life stands in contrast to the way of this world.

And as Jesus made his way toward the temple that day, the folks who fell in behind his parade knew that they were marching in a public protest, a tangible act of opposition to human power and might parading just on the other side of town. They weren't insincere in their following—they knew as they yelled "Hosanna!" that their cries were radical expressions of opposition and defiance.

Perhaps they did not know as they fell in behind him that they would march all the way through the city that week, out into the Garden of Gethsemane, into the courtyards of the most powerful men in society, and eventually up . . . up that hill to crucifixion and death.

But they did know that this was the parade they would join, this strange little band of defiant marchers who preferred not to sing the praises of the powerful but instead to follow the one who dismantled old structures and called for a new world. They held on so tightly to the conviction that hope for the world is not found in human power, but in the way of justice and love, in the way of Christ.

What better story to begin this week, when we will remember what happens when people of faith and good conscience find the courage to confront the biggest and the most powerful forces that work against love, than protest? To resist the powers of this world that close borders and gas innocents and take away health care and send the most vulnerable to detention centers and line the pockets of the excessively wealthy while children in our own country go hungry?

Matthew reports that this little group of faithful protestors sent a loud message in Jerusalem that day. Verse 10 reads: "When he entered Jerusalem, the whole city was in turmoil, asking, 'Who is this?'"

Why?

Because speaking up for what is true and right, even in the face of overwhelming power, has greater impact than we can even begin to imagine. As we set out toward Holy Week, we're invited to decide if we will pick up our palms and our protest signs and join this parade, this protest that is our faith. Because if there's anything we need to remember today, it's this: *we don't even begin living . . . until we find out what we'll die for.*

# 5

# More Bricks, Less Straw

**Kenji Kuramitsu**

Kenji Kuramitsu, a MDiv student at McCormick Theological Seminary in Chicago and an MA in Social Work candidate at the University of Chicago, is the author of *A Booklet of Uncommon Prayer: Collects for the #BlackLivesMatter Movement—and Beyond*. He serves on the board of directors of the Reformation Project, a Christian organization working to advance LGBTQ+ justice, and of the Japanese American Citizens League, the largest and oldest Asian American civil rights group in the United States.

• • •

*Exodus 5:18*

Let me paint the picture for you: fire, rope, sand; shouting, stone, smoke. Heavy strokes, falling on hated flesh, sores festering in the sun, packed in like sardines, far from their native land, serving the whims of hostile masters. "Produce, serve, tear your muscles, expend your children for my purposes," said Pharaoh. "Make more bricks. Use less straw."

A suffering people, a cruel king, and a liberating God: so opens the saga of the Exodus. Those familiar with this story know that this people does not languish in pain forever. God hears the cries of the oppressed, and is moved to redemptive action on their behalf. Yet how exactly did the Hebrew people come to find themselves subjugated in this foreign land?

The preceding book of Genesis concludes with Joseph's royal burial, and the Israelite people living quite happily in Egypt, their land of deliverance from famine and death. Yet Exodus begins with an ominous observation: "[A] new king arose over Egypt, who did not know Joseph" (1:8). This sovereign was inherently distrustful of the Hebrews, and soon after taking office, he begins to sow paranoia: "[T]he Israelite people are more numerous and more powerful than we. Come, let us deal shrewdly with them, or they will increase and, in the event of war, join our enemies and fight against us and escape from the land" (1:9–10).

Soon thereafter, Pharaoh tells his Hebrew subjects that they are lazy, blaming their culture and poor work ethic for their poverty. As additional punishment, he instructs: "Go now, and work; for no straw shall be given you, but you shall still deliver the same number of bricks" (5:18). Mud bricks in this era required straw to give them internal support. To deny these workers access to the necessary raw materials—all while demanding they produce the same amount of end product—amounted to a deepening of their humiliation and bondage.

Many of you are familiar with the Oriental Institute here in Hyde Park. The next time you get the chance, visit the Egyptian wing. Tucked into the northeast corner, at about waist level, is a glass display containing a crude, unremarkable brick. The uneven block is made of silver mud, from which flecks of yellow straw, aged by centuries, peek through the surface. Yet this muddy artifact unleashes my imagination more than all the museum's ancient mummies, ceiling-high statues, and haughty steles combined. This brick, dated to an Egyptian construction project from three thousand years before the birth of Christ, is precisely what the Israelites from our story would have been forced to produce.

Across the mud's top layer, the imperial seal of Ramses II is dimly visible. Ramses the Great gained popular infamy through Yul Brynner's portrayal in the classic film *The Ten Commandments* as the reckless ruler who orchestrated the Israelite's enslavement.[1] The Exodus text does not specify whether the despot in question is indeed this Ramses of history, or of our Hollywood imagination. Yet this magnate's hateful speech is archetypal of the blustery, bombastic demagogues we are familiar with today. Seeding fear and steely policy to fight the presence of phantom traitors in our midst is a well-worn tactic that populist politicians have invoked across the tapestry of our national history.

We are conversant with Pharaoh's breezy hysteria about a "fifth-column" of secret saboteurs operating inside our own borders. I was only eight at the time of the September 11 attacks, but I remember well the fear on the faces around me, the sprawling anxieties about "those people" broadcast into my psyche via television, the pulpit, and peers. Hate crimes, only the most visible tips in the American iceberg of white supremacy, have soared since the election of Donald Trump, and racial scapegoating continues as demographics deepen their shifts and white Americans increasingly resent "feeling like minorities in their own country." At this moment, we are not very far from the racial prejudice, war hysteria, and failure of political leadership of times past.[2]

*If war breaks out, they will join our enemies, fight against us, and then escape from the land.*

On February 18, 1942, with the militarized words of Pharaoh slithering through his mind, President Franklin D. Roosevelt issued Executive Order 9066, setting into motion the largest, most rapid mass incarceration in American history. This legislation cast into chaos more than one hundred twenty thousand Nikkei living across the country's West Coast, inaugurating untold years that will live in infamy.[3]

Imagine waking up that morning and learning that, overnight, your body had become a crime. The black and white posters now hanging on your block broadcast sharp orders to all of Japanese ancestry: Report for mandatory evacuation. No pets will be allowed to travel with you. If you don't have a suitcase, we will give you two trash bags into which to ply your entire life. You have days to sell or stash everything you own while your neighbors, transfigured into sharks and birds of prey, crow with false sympathies lusting for your antiques and acreage.[4]

At the station, see families wearing their Sunday best, the proud faces of elders limping along, infants clinging to mothers and sisters. At gunpoint, each body is fitted with an identification tag, given a number, and shuffled into rasping trains and shuttered buses. Most will be siphoned into hastily-constructed concentration camps throughout the nation's interior, sites swallowed up by heat waves and sandstorms, the way to dusty death.[5]

Despite the thirsty soil, many Nikkei farmers would put their impressive gardening skills to work, eking out thin harvests and sharing their produce with guards and one another. Craftspeople set about making basic furniture without sufficient tools. In such a place, our gardeners and carpenters had to create *ex nihilo* (out of nothing), conjuring green and gear with their own hands.

*No straw will be given to you, but you still need to make the same amount of bricks.*

The Japanese workers who were told to irrigate deserts while behind bars should remind us in some pale way of the losses of those who were forced to labor in this land under pain of death, as well as all prison laborers who today work under legal slavery for mere pittance. We should be reminded of those neighborhoods in Chicago where the state has planted food deserts, architected redlining, disinvested in schools, bestowed crumbling infrastructure, and now summons police on those same neighborhoods like locust plagues to brutally enforce safe and spotless streets.

Yet without proper gardening instruments, without cutting-edge carpentry tools, how can you expect of us wholeness? Pharaoh and his multitudes have stripped us of our straw, stuffed their own mattresses with it, and now demand we produce industrial-grade bricks. It is to the advantage of our rulers when we do not acknowledge this. At one point in the Exodus text, Pharaoh instructs his taskmasters to make the Israelites work so hard that they won't be able to pay attention to his lies (5:9).

In an age daily disoriented by fiction upon fiction, when our trust in public institutions is being purposefully eroded, we often experience certain fatigue when it comes to keeping up with the latest dizzying horror. Imbibing scandal after scandal has the potential to numb us to human suffering, to one another, and to opportunities to resist. Our rulers have tweaked Pharaoh's advice, keeping the poor so hungry, so busy with hard, desperate work, and force-feeding the middle-class bread and circuses and cheap fluorescence, so none of us any longer are able to pay attention to the lies. In such an anesthetized culture, it often takes occasions of extraordinary violence or great courage to shake us back to consciousness.

On the evening of June 19, 1982, a young man named Vincent Chin was celebrating his bachelor's party with friends in a suburb of Detroit. As the night went on, Vincent encountered two white men who, mistaking Chin for Japanese, attacked him, saying "It's because of you little motherfuckers that we're out of work." One assailant held Chin in place while the other cracked open his skull with a baseball bat. Vincent's funeral was held four days later, on the date originally set for his wedding.

Asian Americans have long known that white people believe we all look alike. After Pearl Harbor, some Korean and Chinese Americans even wore buttons identifying themselves as non-Japanese to escape vigilante attacks. Yet after Vincent Chin's murder, many Asian Americans began to take seriously the prospect that we must organize across ethnic lines for our mutual survival. Previously, many of our communities had defined ourselves narrowly, cleaving to insular divisions often carried over from our nations of origin. Now, whether Japanese, Chinese, Cambodian, Filipinx, Thai, or Hmong, many groups realized that we needed to organize together.

At trial, Vincent Chin's killers received a slap on the wrist: probation and a small fine. The judge publicly defended this decision, saying "these weren't the kind of men you send to jail."[6]

What do these "kind of men you send to jail" look like? Perhaps this judge was picturing tattoos and piercings, hoodies and saggy pants, turbans and hijabs. Those who wear badges and carry weapons, as agents of the deeply diseased white American imagination, have historically had a difficult time telling apart friends from enemies. This is why Tamir Rice was murdered for existing on a playground with a toy. It is why Pharaoh swore that the Hebrews in his midst were secret spies. And it is why President Roosevelt and all his men, most of them devout Christians, couldn't tell our frightening yellow faces apart from their enemies across the sea.

To look into the face of the Other and to see a neighbor and a friend has become a rare gift. You may not know the story of Ralph Lazo, who was 16 years old when the government began to round up his Japanese American peers. Lazo's Mexican-Irish descent did not directly implicate him in this saga. When he saw those posters in churches around his neighborhood, Ralph could have stood aside. He could have spread a button on his chest like the blood of a lamb, pleading "I'm not Japanese, this doesn't involve me."

Instead, he was furious. Ralph rejected the idea that those dear to him were "enemy non-aliens." He helped his friends sell their belongings, and accompanied them to the train station on the day of their forced exile. While waving goodbye, urged by his friends' budding requests, Ralph snuck aboard. He traveled to Manzanar concentration camp where he ended up living in the camp barracks, undetected by authorities for several months.[7]

Behind barbed wire, Ralph planted trees. He volunteered as a mailman, held holiday parties and played matchmaker with friends, became a cheerleader at sporting events and was even elected high school class president.

When he was eventually discovered and drafted, Lazo was sent to the Pacific, where he helped his fellow soldiers see the humanity in the Asian faces around them: "The American G.I. couldn't tell the difference between a Japanese and a Filipino," Lazo explained. "That's why they assigned me. [White soldiers] were killing the Filipinos and letting the Japanese go."[8]

Ralph Lazo intuitively recognized the humanity of others, and saw their connection to himself. Asian American communities responding to Vincent Chin's killing came to the realization that we held a shared fate in this land. As one incarcerated prophet phrased it, what affects one of us directly affects all others indirectly because we are "caught in an inescapable network of mutuality, tied in a single garment of destiny."[9] The garment of destiny, that frail raiment of human solidarity, seems at times rather shredded and thin. The litany of woes is long: deportations persist; the worship of whiteness claims human sacrifices and contours the pulpit and the pew; women and nonbinary people are continually crucified under the aegis of patriarchy; communities of color face heightened surveillance and incarceration. The cries of the suffering in this land, across generations, demand deliverance.

In the Exodus text, God's movement on behalf of the Israelites occurs through people, through the wounded healers, those who are willing to risk their lives to stand up for what is right. To this we can say the suffering solidarity of God is realized through acts of human love.

To accompany our childhood friends as they face an inhumane fate. To organize and build coalitions with those we have been taught to distrust. To share our garden produce with our captors, who themselves are more hopelessly bound than us. These are not merely personal acts, but are our sharing in Christ's own victory over the forces of death. God's liberation is not some nebulous affair that occurs passively disconnected from our daily living. God's redeeming work in the universe is furthered by human agents. It's through our hands that barbed wire fences are clipped, that borders are razed, that weapons are pressed into gardening tools.

Pharaoh has gone by many names: Accuser, Caesar, Führer. Czar, Khan, King. Warlord, President, Chief Executive Officer. Yet the rulers of this world and all their friends will shrink away. Their statues to supremacy and confederacy will crumble, their odes to blood and soil will stiffen and fade, their walls of division will go the way of Ramses' temples, swallowed up by silent sands.

Hand in hand, brick by brick, and with sacred song in our heart, we will demand enough straw to make ends meet. We will reject those serpentine lies and sharks mouths that ask us to see our neighbors as less than human. We read these scriptures, we tell these stories, we teach and talk about God's saving role in history and nature because through them we remember what we can become. We were not made to praise false gods and to serve mighty kings, but to dance with our Creator, to serve one another, to delight in this living world in all its glory. We were made for freedom, freedom, freedom.

———

[1]Ramses II was also immortalized in "Ozymandias," a popular sonnet on the ravages of time, by English poet Percy Shelley: "My name is Ozymandias, King of Kings: Look on my works, ye Mighty, and despair!" Public domain, https://www.poets.org/poetsorg/poem/ozymandias.

[2]The Commission on Wartime Relocation and Internment of Civilians concluded in its landmark report "Personal Justice Denied" that "race prejudice, war hysteria, and a failure of political leadership," were the real reasons for the wartime incarceration of Japanese Americans. See the Associated Press's "Excerpts from summary of report on Internments in U.S. in World War II," in *The New York Times,* February 25, 1983, http://www.nytimes.com/1983/02/25/us/excerpts-from-summary-of-report-on-internments-in-us-in-world-war-ii.html.

[3]Nikkei, or *nikkeijin,* are children of the Japanese diaspora.

[4]As Somali poet and refugee activist Warsan Shire has written, "No one leaves home unless home is the mouth of a shark." "Home" became for us, that day, the mouth of a shark. To hear Shire read her poem, see "Home," http://seekershub.org/blog/2015/09/home-warsan-shire/.

[5]Careful to avoid drawing public resonances with the death camps of Nazi Europe, the American government consistently claimed that this mandatory "evacuation" was "for our own safety." My great uncle Clark, a college student at the time of his arrest, never bought this argument. He wondered why, if this prison was for his own protection, the guards always trained their machine guns inside the barbed wire fences.

[6]Mark Tseng-Putterman, "On Vincent Chin and the Kind of Men You Send to Jail," Asian American Writers' Workshop, June 23, 2017, http://aaww.org/vincent-chin-the-kind-of-men/.

[7]In a 1982 interview, Lazo recalled that camp officials couldn't tell him apart from his Nikkei friends: "Being brown has its advantages. . . . Who can say that I haven't got Japanese blood in my veins?"

[8]Cecilia Rasmussen, "Following His Beliefs Led Him to Manzanar," *The Los Angeles Times,* May 27, 2007, http://articles.latimes.com/2007/may/27/local/me-then27.

[9]Martin Luther King Jr., "Letter from a Birmingham Jail," African Studies Center - University of Pennsylvania, https://www.africa.upenn.edu/Articles_Gen/Letter_Birmingham.html.

# 6

# Heresy of Heresies: "From Deadly Unity to Life-Giving Unity"

**José F. Morales Jr.**

Rev. José F. Morales Jr. is the director of pastoral formation at the Disciples Seminary Foundation in Claremont, California, where he's also pursuing a PhD in comparative theology and philosophy at Claremont School of Theology. This sermon was originally delivered in the opening worship service at the General Assembly of the Christian Church (Disciples of Christ) in Indianapolis, Indiana on July 8, 2017. While it focuses on the struggle for unity in the history of the Disciples of Christ, its themes are ubiquitous in a number of denominational traditions with hidden histories of racism and discrimination that also demand to be confronted.

• • •

*John 17:20–23*

Writing this sermon on Christian unity proved to be more difficult than I originally thought. I wasn't sure why. Pressure, expectation, the thought of a jumbotron-size close-up of my head on the convention center's screen . . .

In the midst of praying, studying, writing, throwing away, and rewriting, I wondered why it was so difficult. Eventually, I discovered what it was: preaching on unity is hard, because *unity is hard*. Unity is difficult. It's inconvenient. It's difficult work that rarely materializes fully. Any attempt at a convenient or safe unity is in reality no unity at all.

I think the founders of the Disciples of Christ—who prized the idea of Christian unity more than anything else—were unaware of just how difficult this unity business would be. They may have been a bit optimistic with their millennial aspirations for a Christian union that would usher in the reign of God fully in our midst. But they eventually realized the difficulty at hand, since this unity movement split four times since its inception.[1]

Unity is hard work. It's inconvenient. It's hard because unity *as such* isn't always good. That's right! I said it: unity isn't always good. I know I just uttered the Disciples equivalent of heresy, but there it is. Unity isn't always a good thing. You see, unity is in itself neutral. It can be good or bad. Or, worse yet, it can be bad disguised as good. And in the name of this so-called unity, we Disciples have not only shined; we've also sinned. In the name of this safe unity, we Disciples have ironically been divisive.

Just ask the first Native Americans with whom the first Disciples came in contact. The way the Disciples story is typically told, it would seem that early white-Native contact was minor, if not non-existent. Yet the biblical scholar Jon Berquist, of the Disciples Seminary Foundation, reminded me that the Cane Ridge revivals were conducted in the third most spoken language in that area at the time: English. In 1800, at the time of the revivals, more people in that part of Kentucky spoke Cherokee and French than English. One need only go to scenic Bethany College in West Virginia, where our Disciples Historical Society is lodged, to find several sermons that Barton Stone wrote in Cherokee.

Yet, why no Cherokee Christian Church? We had much contact with Cherokee and other Native and First Nations peoples in those early years, when the zeal for Christian unity was at its most intense. So why didn't we have any noticeable Native leadership early in the movement?

The answer is disturbing. It was because our contact with them was less than Christian, because we didn't include them in the kind of convenient and safe unity we desired. We were even part of the systemic extermination that eventually led to the Trail of Tears and other displacing atrocities. We operated with a notion of unity informed by a "doctrine of discovery," deformed by the nationalism of Manifest Destiny.

True unity was too hard for us so we opted for a safe unity. And in the name of this safe unity, we Disciples have ironically been divisive. After all, any attempt at a safe unity is in reality no unity at all.

Just ask the first African American Disciples, some of whom were there at the beginning, experiencing the revival fire at Cane Ridge. The black evangelistic effort of these first Disciples was relentless and fruitful, giving Walter Scott a run for his money, and leading to sizable growth among African Americans. Black evangelists, like Alexander Campbell (yes, there is another Alexander Campbell in our history), ignited the restoration fire and helped plant churches everywhere they trod.

Yet even before the first battles of the Civil War lit the night sky, many of the white counterparts to these faithful black Disciples remained silent in the face of slavery. Although Campbell (the white Campbell) and Stone denounced the practice, they opted for a safe unity, ignoring the wounded hands and feet of their African American counterparts. In the name of the cross, they turned a blind eye to the lynching tree.[2] This is what safe unity looks like. This is what privileged unity looks like. This is what unfaithful unity looks like.

This safe yet superficial unity by white Disciples led many faithful saints to leave the fold in the last years of the 19th century and the first years of the 20th. Timothy James aptly likens this loss of black leadership in the Disciples to a "mass exodus."[3] And a mass exodus it was. Even as we celebrate the 50th anniversary of the Merger Agreement, let's not forget that this "mass exodus" is the reason the great Preston Taylor started the National Convocation in the first place, that is, to stop the mass withdrawal of faithful women and men who were drawn to the Disciples message of unity but were met by its absence in practice.[4]

Others, like the brilliant Samuel R. Cassius, didn't leave the whole Restoration movement; instead they opted for the less-connected Churches of Christ, so that they wouldn't have to deal with the institutionalized racism in the trans-congregational structure of the church. The eerie indictment of Cassius haunts us still; he criticizes his white colleagues who "preach about the goodness of God, and pray about loving one another, and being one in Christ, but [who] scorn me on account of my race and color, and [who] tell me that their people will not tolerate me as an equal."[5]

True unity, in our racialized reality, was too hard for us, and so we opted for a safe unity instead. Yet, safe unity is no unity at all.

Just ask the Chinese at the end of the 1800s in Portland. Or the Japanese Disciples during World War II. Xenophobic policies in government—materializing in the Chinese Exclusion Act and the internment of Japanese American citizens during World War II—were met, in many places in the established church, by silence or indifference. Safe unity is no unity at all.

Just ask the Latinx communities in Texas in the early 20th century. Time and again, historian Daisy Machado reminds us, they were refused the funding needed to plant new congregations.[6]

Just ask theological conservatives who have been the object of our ridicule, even from General Assembly stages, instead of being treated as faithful partners in theological exploration and debate.

Just ask the LGBTQ+ community, whose intense love for Jesus is somehow insufficient enough, in some parts of our movement, to qualify them for the work of the church. I confess before you all that I'm among those who for years denied their call, and when I accepted it, I remained silent, choosing safe unity instead.

Just ask women, not of yesteryear, but women today, who still—still!—are passed up for men—still!—in the so-called big steeple, prestigious congregations, even when they are often more qualified than their male peers for such a charge.

In the name of this safe unity, we have ironically been the source of division. For safe unity is no unity at all.

In fact, this safe unity kills. It's a safe-yet-deadly unity.

I know it's heresy for a Disciple to say that unity isn't always good. But the greater heresy is division parading as unity. As Preston Taylor declared, such misuse and abuse of "unity" is "the heresy of all heresies."[7]

So, where do we go from here? Should we give up on this unity business altogether?

The unity question is only the first question Christians must ask if we're striving to be one. There's a second unity question that must be raised, and it's this: What kind of unity are we seeking? That is to say, what is the nature of our oneness? What is the ethic or posture from which we strive to be one?

Herein lies the good news of our scripture this evening. Christ's prayer for the church isn't simply for any kind of unity. It's for a specific kind of unity.

> I ask not only on behalf of these, but also on behalf of those who will believe in me through their word, that they may all be one. As you, Father, are in me and I am in you, may they also be in us, so that the world may believe that you have sent me. The glory that you have given me I have given them, so that they may be one, as we are one, I in them and you in me, that they may become completely one. (John 17:20–23)

The unity Christ prays for is demonstrated in his unity with God, whom he calls "Father." Therefore this second question—What kind of unity?—is unavoidably bound to yet another question, and that is: "Who is this Christ who is united with God and who unites us to God and each other?" You see, for John the Evangelist, ecclesiology (who the church is) always corresponds to Christology (who Christ is). In other words, to get at the unity Christ prays for, we need to know something of the Christ who prays for our unity.

Throughout much of church history, this passage was used to develop what would become the doctrine of the Trinity, the belief that God the Mother (a term that some of the Church Fathers did in fact use; it's not some "modern, liberal distortion"[8]) and God the Son are one, that they are (as our scripture reads) "in" each other. They indwell each other, and share and receive completely from each other.

I'm not here to endorse this doctrine of the Trinity, as beautiful as the image of a relational God may be for some of us here. Disciples have never required its affirmation for fellowship. And I for one don't want to start that now. Moreover, when one reads John's Gospel, one recognizes that this doctrine isn't needed to demonstrate how John establishes the unity between Jesus and God. You see, John tells us clearly how such a divine-human unity is realized. A bit earlier in the Gospel, on several occasions, Jesus says that his unity to God is to be proven or seen by works (cf. John

14:10–11).[9] To understand his unity to God, Jesus says, "Look at what I'm doing!"

To get at this unity with God that Christ embodies, and to which Christ call us, we need to look at what he does in the Gospel. And what does Jesus do to demonstrate this unity?

Well, do you remember where this prayer takes place? And do you remember what he is doing in this place? Right before his prayer for unity, Jesus gathers for a meal with his disciples and he washes their feet.

And how about right after the prayer for unity? Where does Jesus go and what does he do? After this prayer for unity, Jesus takes up the cross. Christ's call for unity is bracketed by washing feet and taking up the cross.

What kind of unity are we to live into? What is the posture from which we strive to be one? Based on the works of Christ, true unity requires service and sacrifice. Better yet, true unity is grounded in, and emerges from, service and sacrifice. Between washing feet and taking up a cross.

This isn't safe unity; Christian unity is dangerous and radical.

Vinnetta Golphin, a Disciples minister from Utah, preached an amazing sermon on the foot washing story, concluding that all ministry must be done "at foot level."[10] In other words,

No high pedestal ministry! No greater than thou ministry! No high and mighty ministry!

Ministry—true ministry—is done at foot level.

True unity isn't easy. Dangerous unity is dirty. Radical unity smells like foot funk!

All the previously mentioned abuses and misuses of unity in our Disciples history have one thing in common (and here, I paraphrase the words of Disciples ethicist Toni Bond Leonard): in these safe versions of unity, we Disciples believed that some folks were not even worthy enough to have their feet washed. Yet Jesus demonstrates the contrary by washing the feet of both an imperial tax collector and an anti-imperial insurrectionist, by washing the feet of a betrayer and a beloved. In washing feet, Jesus acknowledged the humanity, the belovedness, of each and all.[11]

This isn't safe unity; it resides between washing feet and taking up the cross. Christian unity is dangerous and radical. This is why earlier in this chapter, Jesus notes that his disciples will be hated by the world (John 17:14).

The radical nature of Christian unity requires some pragmatic nuancing here, especially in light of our history of safe-yet-deadly unity. Here's the caveat: Some folks (in our church and in our world) have been forced to sacrifice themselves for the benefit of a few and forced to serve those few—groups like women, African Americans, the poor, the undocumented, and so on. So we must be clear as to how to speak of sacrifice and service.

Although I disagree with some of her theological conclusions regarding the cross, the womanist theologian Deloris Williams rightly highlights all the ways that "cross," "servant," and "sacrifice" language has been deployed in the oppression of people—especially, she notes, of black female bodies.

Yet the charge to sacrifice and service isn't to force others to empty themselves for our benefit (which is oppressive), but to willingly and vulnerably offer ourselves, through Christ and by the power of the Spirit, for the sake of a broken, divided world. The charge toward radical unity requires that the church as a whole, on its way toward unity, accept these historically rejected bodies, feet and all. This summons necessitates that we simultaneously take up our cross and denounce the ways that our safe unities crucify people every day. Hence, as theologian Jon Sobrino asserts, the charge to take up our cross paradoxically means that we help take the oppressed down from their crosses.[12]

This unity is indeed scandalous. Unity rooted in the ethic of foot washing requires that those of us pampered with institutionalized pedicures and systemic foot rubs be the first on our knees with a water basin and towel in hand. Radical unity requires, at this historical point in our church's life, that some of us sacrifice and serve first and more frequently than others, trusting that in this gospel act of reversal, we will find life—that here, we find the God of life, that "Illimitable Life" (to quote the medieval philosopher Boethius[13]) endlessly shared in love between God the Mother and God's eternal Wisdom, who took on flesh in Jesus of Nazareth.

The paradox and promise of the Gospel is that whereas false unity is safe yet deadly, true unity is dangerous yet life-giving. You see, church, the unity that emerges from a water basin has the power to cleanse us all, for it contains the "living water" that never runs out (cf. John 4:13). The unity that is poured out from shared sacrifice leads to life everlasting because the world built on crosses, lynching trees, and militarized borders is no match for the Risen Christ who shattered the very gates of hell!

Fellow Disciples, let us grow in unity by taking up our shared basin and towel, and let us wash feet—

The feet of the homeless family, whose feet are weary from standing on curbs in search of mercy;

The feet of the Native elder, whose calloused feet tell the story of displacement;

The feet of the undocumented worker, whose wandering feet are scorched by the desert sun;

The feet of the gay teen who is contemplating suicide and whose feet are tired of running from bullies;

The feet of black mothers whose feet can no longer carry the ever-present fear that their children may not come home tonight.

Beloved Disciples, let us take up our shared cross so that we may be one and truly live. Let us take up our shared cross by denouncing a world hopped up on crucifixion. It's between the water basin and the cross where we're truly made one in the Spirit. And it's here, in this radical unity of the Spirit, where we find Jesus, a loving Jesus whose wounded hands wash our feet and whose wounded feet bear the marks of his love. And in finding Jesus, in finding this wounded-yet-risen Christ, we find God, the God of "Illimitable Life," who assures us that there is indeed life on the other side of our sacrifice and service.

---

[1]For a detailed history of the Restoration Movement, see Douglas A. Foster et al., *The Encyclopedia of the Stone-Campbell Movement* (Grand Rapids: Eerdmans, 2012).

[2]Cf. James Cone, *The Cross and the Lynching Tree.*

[3]From personal conversation.

[4]The National Christian Missionary Convention was formed in 1917 by Disciples minister Preston Taylor, a former slave, in order to "empower the witness of Black Disciples as members of the whole church through a partnership with white Disciples that recognized Black leadership in an era of blatant white supremacy and paternalism." In the 1960s, the National Christian Missionary Convention merged with other Disciples organizations. As part of the Merger Agreement in 1968, this led to a new organization called the National Convocation of the Christian Church (see http://disciples.org/our-identity/history-of-the-disciples/).

[5]As quoted by Lawrence Burnley in D. Newell Williams et al., *The Stone-Campbell Movement: A Global History* (St. Louis: Chalice, 2013), 50.

[6]Cf. Daisy Machado, *Of Borders and Margins: Hispanic Disciples in Texas, 1888-1945* (New York: Oxford University Press, 2003).

[7]This quote is from Taylor's speech at the inaugural meeting of the National Convocation in 1917. See Sandhya Jha, *Room at the Table: Struggle for Unity and Equality in Disciples History* (St. Louis: Chalice, 2009), 37.

[8]E.g., Gregory of Nyssa.

[9]Dogmatic note: the Trinity focuses on who Christ is; John in these texts focuses on what Christ does.

[10]Sermon preached at the installation service for Rev. Daphne Gascot Arias, Downey Memorial Christian Church (Disciples of Christ), Downey, CA, January 18, 2015.

[11]Paraphrased from personal conversation.

[12]See Jon Sobrino, *Principle of Mercy: Taking the Crucified People from the Cross* (Maryknoll, NY: Orbis, 2015).

[13]See Boethius, *The Consolation of Philosophy* (Mineola, NY: Dover Publications, 2012).

# 7

# Wake Up and Stay Woke!

**Michael W. Waters**

Rev. Dr. Michael W. Waters is the founding pastor of Joy Tabernacle A.M.E. Church in Dallas. He has appeared on ABC Nightline, BBC Newsnight, CBS This Morning, C-SPAN, MSNBC, NPR, The NBC Nightly News, and PBS Newshour among other media outlets. His books include *Stakes Is High: Race, Faith, and Hope for America*, winner of the 2018 Wilbur Award in Non-fiction, and the forthcoming *As Your Poets Have Spoken: Faith, Hip Hop, and Proclamation*. This sermon was preached at the A.M.E. Annual Conference in Dallas a few weeks before the 2016 general election.

• • •

## *Acts 20:7–12*

The final scene of legendary filmmaker Spike Lee's cinematic classic *School Daze* features "Dap" (a role exquisitely played by the equally legendary Laurence Fishburne), as he sprints across the campus courtyard of the fictional Mission College. After running for some distance and hurdling a wall, Dap finally makes his way to the center of the courtyard. There, the character looks directly into the camera lens to declare an imperative of two words: "Wake up!"

This singular message is repeated by Dap 13 times in less than two minutes during the final three and a half minutes of the film. As Dap continues to shout this refrain from the top of his lungs, the entire campus is stirred from their slumber. Mission students, faculty, staff, and administrators begin to flood into the courtyard, now awake, standing together side by side.

On the 14th and final time of his declaration, with the entire campus surrounding him, Dap offers a slight deviation in his declaration. Dap now offers a plea: "Please, wake up." With these words, the film ends with a still frame, along with the unmistakable accompanying sound of a ringing alarm clock.

It's well-known that being asleep when one should be awake can bring tragic consequences. Falling asleep on the job can quickly result in a termination. Falling asleep in class can quickly result in missing vital information needed in order to pass the course. Falling asleep while operating heavy machinery or while driving a vehicle can prove fatal, not only for an individual, but for those surrounding them. We are even warned against the use of certain medications at certain times as the chemical properties present can make one drowsy and prone to slumber.

What is true in a physical sense is also true in regard to social awareness. Just as it's dangerous to be asleep at certain times, it's also dangerous to be in a social slumber during seasons of critical importance. Being asleep means not being attentive, alert, or active. In times like these, not being attentive, alert, or active can have fatal consequences. It's imperative that we all be awake—or, as stated in the vernacular of these times, that we "Stay woke."

We must stay woke to wealth disparity (the *Wall Street Journal* reported this year that it would take 228 years for the average black family to amass the wealth of an average white family).

We must stay woke politically (there is a presidential nominee whose hatred, racism, and xenophobia won him the endorsement of the Ku Klux Klan).

We must stay woke as it relates to police brutality (although young black men ages 15 to 29 only make up 2 percent of the American population, they account for over 15 percent of all police-related deaths).

We must stay woke as it relates to education. Here in Texas, the state Board of Education is constantly seeking to rewrite history by approving textbooks for our young people that call African slaves unpaid workers, Mexican migrants lazy, and go so far as to suggest that American slavery was really not all that bad.

We must stay woke in Dallas, for while we have the nation's fastest-growing business district, we also lead the nation in childhood poverty for all major cities.

We must stay woke because so many young black men are dying in our city that one news outlet began a series called "Dying in Dallas."

We must stay woke because our Annual Conference is meeting less than two miles from where the FBI claims is the most dangerous intersection in the entire state.

Yet even with all these factors at work, both locally and nationally, I come tonight with an even greater concern: in times like these—when being dormant can have fatal consequences—it often appears as if the church is in a deep slumber. Despite the clear mandate that we stay woke in this world, there is mounting evidence that we are fast asleep.

The church often appears to be asleep to the shifting paradigms of our society and of our world. Twenty-five years before Spike Lee's seminal film was released, a fellow Morehouse man spoke prophetically from a Birmingham jail cell. Armed with only a pen and the margins around a newspaper (and, later, scraps of paper smuggled to him by his attorney),

Rev. Dr. Martin Luther King Jr. penned what is widely considered to be the greatest treatise on nonviolent philosophy and resistance in the 20th century. From his masterful text, we inherit such powerful quotations as "Injustice anywhere is a threat to justice everywhere. We are caught in an inescapable network of mutuality, tied in a single garment of destiny. Whatever affects one directly, affects all indirectly." But even more compelling than King's words in defense of nonviolent resistance are King's words in critique of the church:

> The contemporary church is so often a weak, ineffectual voice with an uncertain sound. It's so often the arch supporter of the status quo. Far from being disturbed by the presence of the church, the power structure of the average community is consoled by the church's often vocal sanction of things as they are.

> But the judgment of God is upon the church as never before. If the church of today does not recapture the sacrificial spirit of the early church, it will lose its authentic ring, forfeit the loyalty of millions, and be dismissed as an irrelevant social club with no meaning for the twentieth century. I meet young people every day whose disappointment with the church has risen to outright disgust.[1]

Two years after his "Letter from Birmingham Jail," in his June 1965 commencement address at Oberlin College, Dr. King recounted the mythological story of *Rip Van Winkle,* who was asleep for 20 years and slept through the entire American Revolutionary War. To this, Dr. King stated, "There are all too many people who, in some great period of social change, fail to achieve the new mental outlooks that the new situation demands. There is nothing more tragic than to sleep through a revolution."[2]

Later, at the National Cathedral in Washington, D.C., in 1968, Dr. King elaborated on this theme: "One of the great liabilities of history is that all too many people fail to remain awake through great periods of social change. Every society has its protectors of status quo and its fraternities of the indifferent who are notorious for sleeping through revolutions. Today, our very survival depends on our ability to stay awake, to adjust to new ideas, to remain vigilant and to face the challenge of change."[3]

Unfortunately, however, we live in a time when Dr. King's worries about the church have largely come true. I dare say that the contemporary church can rightly be called protectors of the status quo and fraternities of the indifferent, for people are literally dying at our doorstep, but we are doing nothing about it.

Furthermore, we are losing entire generations. We have churches dying in cities although they are surrounded by people on every side. Most young adults today consider the church to be a nonfactor in engaging the critical struggles in times like these. Many consider the church as being more consumed with preserving its history and traditions than fighting for justice and improving the daily lives of people. Many young people view the church in the same light as another one of the most important voices of the 20th century, Tupac Amaru Shakur, who called churches "ghetto mansions"—pretty to look at on the outside, but doing nothing for their community. Our nation is in the midst of another revolutionary time for racial justice and equality, but it often appears as if the church is asleep at the wheel.

For far too many years, as our people were being brutalized by police violence, the church has been silent.

For far too many years, as Congress stripped away the Voting Rights Act, the church has been silent.

For far too many years, as the war on drugs and the prison industrial complex re-enslaved our black masculinity—and now, with rapidly increasing numbers, our black femininity—the church has been silent.

Just as problematically, when people begin to speak out for justice today, the church is often the first to criticize and condemn their actions. Just look at the discrepancy in the ways that the church responds to situations of violence in the city of Dallas.

Collette Flanagan and her organization, Mothers Against Police Brutality, note that over 60 families in Dallas today are working through her organization to seek answers to the questionable deaths of their loved ones at the hands of Dallas police officers.[4] Until a black police officer was indicted by a grand jury earlier this month for killing a Latinx youth, it had been over 40 years since any police officer had been indicted in the murder of a citizen in Dallas. Over the course of all this time—40 years of death and destruction—the church has largely been silent. No, the church has been dormant—*asleep.*

While there have been nonviolent protests, marches, and demonstrations for years that call attention to this violence, the church has been asleep, hard to find, failing to speak up and resist. But this past summer, as soon as one lone and deranged gunman tragically opened fire on police after another rally and march in Dallas had ended peacefully and without incident (people were already going home), all of a sudden many in the church started to condemn the nonviolent protestors. They asked us, "Why were you out there, anyway?"

Well, let me tell you why we were out there: We were out there because our people are dying daily in the streets for selling CDs, missing a traffic signal, and playing their music too loud. It doesn't matter if we're standing with our hands up or lying down on the ground, we can still be shot by police. That's why we're out there. And the church should care as much about this violence as any other form of violence. When the church doesn't, it's deeply troubling. And revealing.

In times like these, when the church is needed the most, the church is slumbering. And a wake-up call is undeniably in order. It's time for the alarm clock to ring.

In our text, we find evidence of the tragedies that befall us all when the church is asleep. But we also find hope for what happens when the church wakes up. The apostle Paul was preaching in Troas, a seaport city and Roman province in Asia where he had stayed for a week after arriving by ship from Philippi. Because he was leaving the next day, the Bible says that Paul preached all day long, all the way to midnight.

Surely Paul had an important message. And it's undeniable that Paul possessed a sharp theological mind. But in this text, it appears as if neither Paul nor the church gathered around him did well in discerning the time. And even good things done at the wrong time can have fatal consequences.

Paul preached so long that candles had to be lit in the upstairs room to provide some light. The Bible says that a young man named Eutychus was sitting on the windowsill on the third floor. As he sat there, Paul kept going on and on. And Eutychus became so drowsy that he fell into a deep sleep. While he was asleep, Eutychus fell out of the window and plunged to his death, three stories down.

It would be easy to condemn Eutychus for his own death. We could say that he never should've sat on the windowsill. We could say he shouldn't have fallen asleep in church. We could say he has no one to blame but himself.

But you can't condemn Eutychus if you don't look at his environment.

Here is a young man dwelling on the edge. Here is a young man sitting for hours upon the brink of disaster. Here is a young man perilously close to tragedy. But no one in the church said a word. Not the preacher. Not the ushers. Not the saints gathered there. No one invited him down and made room for him on the floor. And although he was present with them, no one paid enough attention to him to know he was getting sleepy. They only take notice of him after he succumbed to his environment.

Too often, the church only takes notice of people who are living on the edge after tragedy befalls them. This in itself is a great tragedy.

While this young man is the one who fell asleep, I declare that it was the church that needed to stay woke. The church was so consumed with itself it forgot about those on the margins living in danger. The church was so consumed with itself it carried on for hours but never moved the people into action. The church was so consumed with itself it allowed a young man to die on its watch.

As a matter of fact, one Bible scholar states that his environment contributed directly to his condition because since the room contained many lamps and people, it stands to reason that oxygen levels were low. It was low enough for everyone present to be a bit lightheaded. The lack of oxygen present could have been enough to cause young Eutychus to sit in the window. How many young people today are sitting in the window because a slumbering church is suffocating them?

There is some good news in the text. There is some hope in the text. It's found in Eutychus' name. His name in Greek means "good fortune"—or, we might say, lucky.

The Bible says that Paul went down, bent over Eutychus, took him in his arms and told everybody not to worry, for the boy was alive. Then they went up and shared in the Lord's Supper. Paul spoke life into a dead situation, and a dead situation came back to life. For this is what happens when the church is woke.

But we know that Eutychus was not simply lucky. He was a blessed child of God. We, too, should be able to declare that despite all the times we have sat on the edge, despite all the times we have been in perilous situations, despite all the fatal situations that we have faced, we are still blessed for we are still God's children.

What was true then is true now:

When the church is woke, new life comes to dead situations and overcomes fatal circumstances.

When the church is woke, the captives are set free.

When the church is woke, signs and wonders follow.

When the church is woke, healing and deliverance take place.

When the church is woke, the people are not condemned, but they are empowered.

Church, in times like these, we must wake up! And stay woke!

---

[1] For the full text of Martin Luther King's letter, see "Letter from a Birmingham Jail," https://kinginstitute.stanford.edu/king-papers/documents/letter-birmingham-jail.

[2] For the 1965 version of Martin Luther King Jr.'s speech at Oberlin College, see "Remaining Awake through a Great Revolution," http://www2.oberlin.edu/external/EOG/BlackHistoryMonth/MLK/CommAddress.html.

[3] For the 1968 version of Martin Luther King Jr.'s speech, see "Remaining Awake through a Great Revolution," http://kingencyclopedia.stanford.edu/encyclopedia/documentsentry/doc_remaining_awake_through_a_great_revolution/.

[4] Learn more about Mothers Against Police Brutality online at http://mothersagainstpolicebrutality.org/.

# 8

# Take a Knee

**Lori Walke**

Lori Walke serves as the associate minister at Mayflower Congregational United Church of Christ in Oklahoma City, Oklahoma, where this sermon was preached on October 1, 2017. The immediate backdrop of the sermon is two-fold: First, it follows President Trump's comments denigrating NFL players who chose to take a knee during the national anthem as part of their nonviolent protest against police violence and racism. Second, it was preached on the Sunday that Mayflower Church held a congregational vote on whether or not to be in solidarity with undocumented immigrants by joining the Sanctuary Movement.[1]

• • •

*Philippians 2:1-13*

When I read the text for this Sunday, my first thought was that the Revised Common Lectionary was trolling President Trump. Trolling is a technical term that describes behavior that is intentionally provocative or offensive. While the lectionary readings were developed decades ago, what are the odds that in the same week President Trump condemns black NFL players for protesting systemic racism by taking a knee during the national anthem, we are *also* asked to study scripture that includes the phrase, "every knee shall bow"?

Oh, President Trump, you're just making this too easy. Just looking at the last seven days, he's called black professional athletes who are protesting crude names, implied that Puerto Rico's hurricane-devastated people are too lazy to participate in clean-up efforts, and alluded to San Juan mayor Carmen Cruz as "nasty" after she asked him to start acting like the most powerful man in the world—because he *is* that man, if only he was actually interested in being the president of the United States. I can't tell that he is. So yeah, I really thought the lectionary was trolling President Trump, offering up scripture on which to preach about humility and servanthood.

But he'd probably never hear that sermon, and I hate to waste a good sermon. I think my chances of being invited to preach at the White House are about as high as my chances of being invited back to the Oklahoma State House to offer another prayer.[2] Besides, such a sermon would be disingenuous. To act like President Trump is an exception to American culture is to pretend that his behavior isn't enabled by the misogyny, racism, and xenophobia we act out every day on our smaller stages. If we want to live in a world where it's impossible for a person to be elected president after bragging about sexually assaulting women, then the rest of us are going to have to refuse to engage in "harmless" benevolent sexism— like telling a woman she's too pretty to be a preacher.

Maybe one day I'll get to preach to President Trump, but you're stuck with me until then. (Unless I offend enough of you today, but I doubt that will happen. This congregation doesn't expect to be offered baby food from the pulpit.)

So here we are, on the edge of a congregational meeting and congregational vote to discern how we as a church will respond to the crisis faced by our undocumented neighbors, who are threatened by heightened ICE activities and oppressed by unjust immigration policy. Although it has always been unjust, for some of us the brokenness of our immigration system was first brought to our attention in January of this year when President Trump issued an executive order named "Protecting the Nation from Foreign Terrorist Entry into the United States," which barred admission to the United States for all people from seven countries (Iraq, Iran, Libya, Somalia, Sudan, Syria, and Yemen) for 90 days, as well as entry to all refugees from anywhere in the world for 120 days, and placed an indefinite ban on refugees from Syria (while at the same time we were dropping bombs on them).

The Sunday after that executive order was issued, I preached a sermon about how refugee and immigration policy is a matter of hospitality for Christians. Half of that sermon was simply a reading of scripture—in part because you can take the girl out of the Baptist church, but you can't take the Baptist church out of the girl—but mostly because it demonstrated that the Bible is unequivocal in its instructions on how we are to treat the stranger.

I proposed that this congregation consider joining the Sanctuary Movement,[3] and pledge to resist the administration's executive orders and policy proposals that target undocumented immigrants and refugees. I asked that we dedicate ourselves to educate and activate, to amplify and respond to the voices of immigrant leaders, and to speak out against the discrimination of any and all marginalized people. I asked that we get ready to open the doors of our sacred space and accompany those facing deportation. I said then and will say again now that I believe Mayflower Church should be a sanctuary church, both on paper and in practice.

Our response to our unjust immigration policy is not based *only* on the biblical "welcome mat mandate" that compels us to offer hospitality. It's also that unjust immigration policy is about racial discrimination, an evil Christians are compelled to battle as a matter of faith. Like other uncomfortable truths, American history textbooks ignore this point or explain it away as necessary to protect American workers, who of course always happen to be white. Since the beginning, our country has used race and ethnicity to determine who can come, who can work, and who can stay.[4] The law student in me had to write and rewrite the following explanation to keep it reasonable in length, but even though I wanted to keep it brief, the history of racism in this country is long: the 1790 Naturalization Act excluded nonwhite people from eligibility to naturalize (the process by which immigrants become citizens). The specific requirements for naturalization were two years of residence in the country, "good moral character," and the applicant must be a "free white person."

In 1882, Congress passed the Chinese Exclusion Act, which banned Chinese laborers from immigrating for the following 10 years. The 1917 Immigration Act banned immigration from most Asian countries, except the Philippines (which was a U.S. colony) and Japan, because they had voluntarily ended a worker immigration program on their own. The Immigration Act of 1924 continued the ban on immigration from Asia, and further laid out the following hierarchy: "Northern Europeans are a superior subspecies of the white race. The Nordics were superior to the Alpines, who in turn were superior to the Mediterraneans, and all of them were superior to the Jews and the Asians."[5] Prior to 1965, residents of only three countries, Ireland, Germany, and the United Kingdom (all overwhelmingly white), were given nearly 70 percent of the visas available to enter the United States. The policy was clear: white people in, brown people out.

Finally, in 1965, Congress passed a law that undid national origin quotas, instead opting for a system that allocated visas equally across countries with an annual limit per country. While good intent was certainly present, this policy closed our country's doors to our closest neighbors—people in Mexico and Latin America—creating the need for them to immigrate illegally, which in turn led to a militarized border.[6]

In theory, the new approach created a "fair" system in which each nation had the same level of access to the same number of U.S. visas each year. But of course *fair* is not the same as *just*. In practice, the new system, among other things, did not acknowledge the reality of the already well-established migratory flow between Mexico and the United States. When opportunities for legal entry closed up on our border with Mexico, the previous flow of immigrants was quickly reestablished under unauthorized auspices. Faced with the significant risks of crossing the border, after first entering the United States, Mexican and Latin American immigrants hunkered down to stay, dramatically reducing the rate of out-migration, while the rate of in-migration continued at a high rate as people turned to the United States for economic opportunity and escape from violence. As migrant workers spent more time north of the border, unable to travel legally, their spouses and children increasingly migrated to the United States to join them. As such, U.S. law and policy created and continues to exacerbate the conditions that force illegal immigration.

So what does all this have to do with Paul and the church in Philippi? I haven't forgotten the scripture lesson. It's important to remember that the short excerpt we read belongs in the context of a longer letter, the purpose of which is set out earlier in the text. Paul is writing, in part, because the church in Philippi is facing conflict. Based on some of the hints in the first chapter, biblical scholars believe that the church was under the threat—if not the reality—of arrest for noncompliance with the government.[7]

And now it feels like the lectionary is trolling Mayflower Church. We did not consult the lectionary when we called a congregational meeting for this date. But really, what are the odds that in the same week we call a congregational vote that includes the option to protest injustice in such a way that might lead to arrest, we are also asked to study scripture about a church facing the choice to either conform to the status quo or be arrested?

Pastor Paul reminds the church of the tools in their tool box: "If there is any encouragement in Christ, any consolation from love, any sharing in the Spirit, any compassion and sympathy" (Phil. 2:1), but it's a bit concealed by the use of the word "if," which for us most commonly expresses uncertainty. But this type of conditional clause was used to lay a foundation for a request, so that it should read, "*Since* there is encouragement in Christ, *since* there is consolation from love, *since* there is sharing in the Spirit, *since* there is compassion and sympathy . . ." Paul tells them to use their most powerful resources: the example of Jesus, love, partnership, compassion, and sympathy.

Then he reminds them to check their worst demons: selfish ambition, concept, and self-interest, instead putting on the mind of Jesus—who might be described as taking a knee to protest systemic oppression. For Paul, "every knee shall bow" was a political statement about who the church owed allegiance to, which was *not* Caesar. It's not apparent that the church in Philippi was locked in a Christological debate, so it seems that Paul was simply reminding the church that discipleship has a cost, one that our teacher Jesus paid for with his life. Faithful to teaching, preaching, and living the kingdom of God; faithful unto death. Not just faithful until it got difficult. Not just faithful until the threat of arrest. Faithful unto death. This was the mindset of Jesus.

Finally, Paul reminds them that salvation is not as easy as saying some magic words, but must rather be worked out with fear and trembling. Fear and trembling—what we might define as careful discernment with the faithful-unto-death mindset of Jesus.

White Christian moderates (to borrow a phrase from Martin Luther King Jr.) often ask for more time to study the issue, but then rarely set themselves to the task of studying the issue (ask me how many Mayflower members attended the White Privilege workshops last fall) and even less often move from education to action, instead letting black and brown bodies shoulder the brunt of injustice and bear the physical and emotional cost not only of the discriminatory policies themselves, but also the cost of protesting discrimination. Requesting "more time to study the issue" is the language of the privileged. Let's study the effects of separate-but-equal a little longer, said no black person ever. Migrant farm workers from Mexico are not asking for a deeper look at labor practices in America.

So this is our task today—to work out our salvation with fear and trembling—to decide *how we will account for our response* to the crisis faced by our undocumented neighbors. I will close by quoting Mayflower's own constitution, because along with those things Paul named (example of Jesus, love, partnership, compassion, and sympathy), it will guide us in taking the next faithful step.

Mayflower Congregational United Church of Christ:

> The purpose of this Church is to seek the transcendent mystery we call God, to interpret and proclaim the gospel of Jesus Christ for our time, to respond to the work of the Spirit, to model inclusiveness and unconditional love, and to seek peace through *justice* for all of creation.

> We do not seek a congregation defined by orthodoxy, but rather a collection of disciples united by orthopraxy—responding in our daily lives to the love of God as revealed through the life, death, and resurrection of Jesus of Nazareth. We wish to create a beloved community that practices an extravagant welcome, gives generously to others the grace we have so generously received, and resists by the power of love those forces in the world that separate, oppress or deny freedom and dignity to all people. Our faithfulness will not be measured by the purity of our beliefs, but by how well we do justice, love kindness, and walk humbly in the ways of Jesus.

I actually don't think the lectionary is trolling Mayflower Church. I have a hunch it's the Holy Spirit, offending our self-righteous sensibilities and provoking us to practice what we profess.

So then, church, shall we be comfortable? Or shall we be faithful?

• • •

For interested readers, here's some background information that describes the process that guided Mayflower in this process, as well as how the congregation voted.

Mayflower prepared for this vote over a period of 10 months, holding two congregational meetings that included hearing from Dreamers and immigration attorneys, as well as watching the Church Insurance Board's webinar on Sanctuary Churches as a congregation during the Sunday school hour. They also encouraged congregants to attend events sponsored by Dream Act of Oklahoma and the Oklahoma Conference of Churches.

On the Sunday of the vote, here's what the ballot looked like:

- A. Do nothing as this time, with the understanding that we will study the issue further, and consider engaging in some or all activities listed under options B and C.
- B. Declare Mayflower to be a Sanctuary Church, with the understanding that this includes, in addition to activities listed in Option C, a willingness to use our church building as a short- or long-term residence to shield individuals and families from deportation action, and knowingly transporting undocumented immigrants. This action can lead to the arrest of those responsible on felony charges.
- C. Declare that Mayflower is joining the Sanctuary Movement, with the understanding that this includes a willingness to meet basic human needs for all people, without regard to immigration status. Joining the sanctuary movement also means: 1) offering material support to sanctuary churches, 2) giving priority meeting space for legal clinics and immigration rights organizations, 3) creating safe space for temporary shelter during heightened ICE activity, 4) exploring the possible use of financial resources to assist individual immigrants and their families, and 5) coordinating with immigrant rights organizations to be a resource for "underground" efforts.

Here are the results of the vote:

A. 12

B. 128

C. 63

---

[1]More details on how the Mayflower congregation prepared for this vote, as well as the results of it, can be found as an addendum to this sermon.

[2]For the full text of her prayer and blessing, see the official Oklahoma House Journal for Thursday, April 13, 2017, https://www.okhouse.gov/Journals/HJ2017/2017%20HLeg%20Day39.pdf, 890–91.

[3]For details on the Sanctuary Movement, see http://www.sanctuarynotdeportation.org.

[4]For a brief summary of this history, see http://www.pewhispanic.org/2015/09/28/selected-u-s-immigration-legislation-and-executive-actions-1790-2014/.

[5]Stephen Klineberg, as quoted in Jennifer Ludden, "1965 Immigration Law Changed Face of America," *National Public Radio,* May 9, 2006, http://www.npr.org/templates/story/story.php?storyId=5391395.

[6]Much of the information in these paragraphs relies heavily on the succinct-but-thorough article by Douglas S. Massey, "How a 1965 immigration reform created illegal immigration," in *The Washington Post,* September 25, 2015, https://www.washingtonpost.com/posteverything/wp/2015/09/25/how-a-1965-immigration-reform-created-illegal-immigration/?utm_term=.1a2ad94cdd4d.

[7]Fred Craddock, *Philippians* (Louisville: Westminster John Knox, 2011), 34.

# 9

# Sinking: A Sermon in the Wake of Charlottesville

**Austin Crenshaw Shelley**

Rev. Austin Crenshaw Shelley is the associate minister for Christian education at the Presbyterian Church of Chestnut Hill in Philadelphia, Pennsylvania, where this sermon was preached on August 13, 2017, the first Sunday after the "Unite the Right" white nationalist rally in Charlottesville, Virginia. Earlier in the worship service, she shared the following words to set up her sermon:

I ask of you a moment of personal privilege. As Head of Staff, Cynthia Jarvis could have insisted on preaching today, even though I was on the schedule. She could have, and she probably wanted to, because any preacher worth her salt wants to be in the pulpit today speaking love in the face of hate. Instead, she has chosen, however reluctantly or unwisely, to trust me with a word that must be spoken. I'm grateful for that trust, and for your trust, and for the gospel which has been entrusted to all of us as people of faith . . . I take the liberty to remind you of something [Cynthia] has said in the past—that a pastor's role in preaching, like the shepherd's staff, is twofold. Sometimes sermons draw you near and bring comfort. Sometimes they prod and agitate. This sermon falls in the latter category. It is intentionally provocative. It may make you uncomfortable or even angry. I'm not flippant about that; all I ask is that you hear me out, and I promise to afford you the same courtesy should you want to remain in conversation. I believe our relationship as a family of faith can hold that tension.

• • •

*Genesis 37:1–4, 12-28; Matthew 14:22-33*

The snout of the Athabasca Glacier in the Canadian Rocky Mountains is just a few hundred yards away from Icefields Parkway, a stunning, scenic route between Banff and Jasper National Parks in the province of

Alberta. When our family stopped to see the glacier just a few weeks ago, I underestimated the reflection of the sun off the ice and sustained a wicked sunburn. So I brought back from Canada souvenir tan lines that prove my lack of good judgment. But what has stuck with me even more than the sunburn is the memory of small historical markers along the walking trail leading to the glacier's edge. I might have missed the first one on the far side of the parking lot just off the highway, except that my four-year-old was climbing on it. No more than two feet high, and definitely off the beaten path, the stone marker blended into the background. It simply said, "The glacier was here in 1843." As we hiked toward the glacier's edge on a trail of rock and rubble left behind by the glacier itself as it has receded, I noticed more of these markers—off to the side, unobtrusive, and yet still quietly telling the sad truth that the glacier is receding at an alarming and accelerating rate.

"The glacier was here in 1908," read the marker at the foot of the path. A ways later, "The glacier was here in 1925." Then "The glacier was here in 1935." We walked on, sometimes slipping and stumbling on the rocks left in the glacier's wake. "The glacier was here in 1942." We helped the children on the steepest parts of the climb. "The glacier was here in 1982." By the time we reached the marker showing where the glacier was in 1992, the message these markers conveyed was growing painfully clear. At the 1992 marker, we were only about halfway from the parking lot to the glacier's current position. You're probably already doing the math. In the last 25 years, the glacier has moved roughly the same distance it had moved in the previous 149 years.

I could go on about shrinking glaciers and the truth they tell us about the damage we are doing to the environment God has entrusted to our care, but that is a sermon for another day. Because what I must name today is the myth my privilege once allowed me to believe. There was a time not so long ago when I could believe that racism in this country was something like that glacier. Sure, it still existed in the distance. I could easily see and even trip over the rough terrain, the scars it had left behind, but it was receding, or so I thought. There was a time when I could sit in the comfort of an American history class, watching black and white reel to reel films of the Ku Klux Klan. I could see blurry footage of men on horseback, clad in bed sheet hoods and carrying torches as they terrorized communities, burning crosses on lawns and lynching black lives—and I could regard those films as shameful, horrific scenes, relics from a backward and terrifying time in this country's past. Though I've known for some time now that racism is alive and well and thriving, I confess with sorrow that I didn't realize soon enough that the vitriol of those earlier days has never disappeared, nor has it retreated. I'm not naive enough to be surprised by the events of yesterday and Friday night in Charlottesville, Virginia, but I'm horrified anew as I'm unmistakably reminded once more that the marker for racism in 2017 is in the exact same spot as it was in the 1950s and '60s. I don't mean to minimize the torture of those who endured the rage of white supremacists then, but I worry it may yet be possible that history will show that things may be getting worse. Klan members now feel free to carry torches in broad daylight and see no need for fashioning bed sheets into hoods to mask their identities. Indeed, they can openly carry weapons and act as a de facto security force for so-called "protesters" who are, if we are being as honest as we should be, hate-filled domestic terrorists. I hope in light of yesterday's events that we have all considered how different would be the fate of black or brown men (non–law enforcement) openly carrying weapons under similar circumstances.

I don't have to tell you that a storm is raging. You can pick that up from whatever news outlet you favor. I'm no journalist. As a pastor, I'm not called to give you a rundown of the news. My call is to preach the truth and the hope of gospel as it speaks into the events of our lives.

The truth is, we are sinking.

Yesterday a colleague of mine who responded to the clergy call in Charlottesville was harassed by white supremacists as she walked to her car after everyone was asked to disperse. She wrote to a group of our colleagues, "It became apparent very quickly that I was not safe. I encountered a large, very loud, all male group of white supremacists who were looking for a confrontation. The police officer and legal observers watching were not a deterrent. . . . [I]n broad daylight, in a bustling city full of police officers and legal observers and volunteers . . . I encountered armed white supremacists."[1] My colleague is thankfully safe in her home, preaching this morning to her congregation, but she is lucky. One young person[2] who was there to speak love into the face of hate was killed when a car drove into a crowd of people who had been peaceably protesting the "Unite the Right" rally. At least 19 people were injured by that car, and the number of people who are reported to have been injured in Charlottesville continues to rise.

*We are sinking.* We are in a pit, well on our way to being imprisoned by the powers of this world. Like Joseph, we have brought it on ourselves to be sure; those of us in positions of privilege have been wearing that privilege like a robe with long sleeves. Like Joseph we are responsible, but neither are we entirely to blame. That robe was handed to us not because we deserved it, but because our lives were seen as more valuable than other lives. We are culpable and simultaneously ensnared in a system in which hatred of those who differ from us, who are not as privileged as we are, is as old as time.

*We are sinking.* The boat we thought was sturdy is being tossed around like it's made of popsicle sticks. We are being shown just how frail, how thin the veneer between us and the storm waged by hate really is. Not only are we inside the storm; the storm has made its way inside us.

*We are sinking.* White supremacists spout Nazi slogans like "Blood and soil," yet our president—who is characteristically unapologetic about offending people—goes out of his way not to offend white supremacists or to implicate their actions as evil. With the same lips that threaten nuclear war as if it's a game of chicken, the leader of our nation generically condemns "hatred, bigotry, and violence on many sides," instead of specifically condemning the actions of domestic terrorists. Never before have I so deeply questioned what year this is. Never before have I been so confused about who we are. Never before have I so fervently prayed for the soul of our country.

I'm well aware that I have just agitated approximately half of you. I pause here to clarify that if you think this sermon is about politics, you are mistaken. Our political stances and the deep divisions they cause are symptoms of an underlying illness. They both reflect and impact the way we treat other people—the way we *other* people. This sermon is not *about* politics. This sermon is about whether we today have more or less capacity than our predecessors to look into the face of our neighbors and see in them the beloved image of God.

*We are sinking.* As the storm rages about us, will we be able, with integrity, to recite and to live the words of the Belhar Confession (written in Afrikaans in 1982 and recently adopted by the Presbyterian Church [USA]), which says in part, "We reject any doctrine which . . . sanctions in the name of the gospel or of the will of God the forced separation of people on the grounds of race and color and thereby in advance obstructs and weakens the ministry and experience of reconciliation in Christ"?[3]

*We are sinking.* Will we have the faith of Rev. Traci Blackmon, a black woman who preached a sermon yesterday in Charlottesville inside a church that was surrounded by white supremacists—surrounded to the extent that law enforcement deemed it unsafe for the worshippers inside to exit the building?

*We are sinking.* Will we have the sheer guts of the students who stood peaceably protesting hate even as they were encircled by torch-carrying, weapon-toting white supremacists?

*We are sinking,* and this is not our only storm. Some of you have lost loved ones this week and in weeks past. Some of you mourn the loss of loved ones long ago. Some of you are exhausted from seeking employment, others are scarred by estrangement from family or friends. For others, your health or the health of those you love is in the midst of the storm. Whatever your storm, and however inconvenient more wind and waves might seem, *this* storm in which we all find ourselves today, day one after Charlottesville, demands our immediate attention and our immediate action.

I began this sermon by telling you about the markers at Athabasca Glacier, the small, easily overlooked monuments to the glacier's receding movement. What I have not told you is that there are also large signs at Athabasca. Warning signs that cannot be missed. Signs that come more frequently as one nears the glacier's edge. They say things like: "Hold fast to your children," "Many have died here," "Don't cross the barriers," "There are no rescue missions when children fall into crevasses, only recoveries," and "Hypothermia will kill small children who fall into the ice before our expert recovery teams can reach them."

Even closer to the snout of the glacier are memorials for those who have slipped into the crevasses—several toddlers and small children, a nine-year-old boy whose story I remember because he died the very day Mark and I were married. The memorials include even a handful of older children and adults who fell into impossible to see cracks in the ice and froze to death despite the warnings.

The journey ahead of us—ahead of Charlottesville—is treacherous, the crevasses hidden, the consequences deadly. More deadly, in fact, for our brothers, sisters, and siblings who are targeted by hate groups than for most of us in this room. Watch your step. Hold fast to the children. Many have died here. The edge of the glacier is right here, just where it's always been. And it's not moving, at least not anytime soon. If we are going to put distance between the ugly disease of racism in this country and us, we are going to have to stand at its edge, stare it down, and forbid it to come any closer or to claim the lives of any more children.

The storm is as strong as ever. We are sinking. But the hope of the gospel is this: if we are willing, the one who walks on the waves—the one who is unmoved by the storm—will command us to do the impossible—to get out of the boat we've been clinging to—to abandon the vessel, the privilege we thought would protect us—and to trust him instead. If we are willing to get our feet wet doing the work of justice; if we are willing to struggle toward Jesus knowing we don't have what it takes to reach him; if we are willing to call upon the only one who can save us when we falter, I believe we will find ourselves firmly within his grasp. In the meanwhile, may we have the good sense to pray as Peter did, this day and every day, "Lord, save us."

---

[1]As shared by Allison Unroe on her personal Facebook page, August 12, 2017.
[2]The victim of the car attack was later revealed to be Heather D. Heyer, age 32.
[3]See "The Belhar Confession," https://www.pcusa.org/site_media/media/uploads/theologyandworship/pdfs/the_belhar_confession-rogers.pdf.

# 10

# Overcome Evil with Good

---

**Jin S. Kim**

Rev. Dr. Jin S. Kim is the founding pastor of Church of All Nations (PCUSA) in Columbia Heights, Minnesota, adjunct professor at the University of Dubuque Theological Seminary, and founder of Underground Seminary. He grew up in the Deep South after emigrating from Korea with his family at age seven. This reflection was shared at Church of All Nations on September 3, 2017. (Editor's note: this is an edited transcript produced from an audio recording; some phrases and quotes are paraphrased. Rev. Kim prefaces his remarks by updating the congregation on his sabbatical, which he had just completed. He then turns his attention to how the church might respond to some of the events that took place while he was on sabbatical, which is where this chapter begins.[1])

• • •

*Romans 12:9–21*

There was a lot going on in Korea this past summer [where Rev. Kim spent part of his sabbatical], and North Korea continues to be in the news here. That's alarming to me because the shape of our national discourse keeps adding one group to hate and fear after another. Just last week North Korea launched a missile over Japan. That's an incredibly provocative act, given our histories and our geopolitics. And if the present administration decides to react through military measures, and Pyongyang responds, things could go very badly, and lots of innocent people will be swept up in it.

Just a few Saturdays ago, as we were driving to Atlanta, the events in Charlottesville started to unfold. We know we've had white supremacist groups in this country throughout our whole history—hundreds if not thousands of them all over the country—in every single state.

What's new about Charlottesville, however, is that they didn't feel the need to hide inside a hood. They didn't feel a need to do their military

66

marches in rural Idaho or Georgia or Arkansas, but right in the shadow of our nation's capital, right next to and through the University of Virginia, founded by Thomas Jefferson himself and considered one of the elite, liberal southern colleges in this country. And with the whole world watching, over a thousand people boldly showed the world their intentions—intentions that are nothing short of genocide.

On the one hand we could say, "Okay, thankfully, they're just a thousand people, and there are many more people who are opposed." But when you have a small group that is truly committed to a cause, and are willing to die for it, and the vast majority of people against them are not willing to put themselves on the line—well, that's exactly the recipe that was at work in Nazi Germany. There were very few Nazis. And they weren't popular. Most of Germany in the early 1930s was viewed as a progressive, liberal nation. In just about every area of human endeavor in the European context, whether it was music or the arts or theater or academics, theology or philosophy or science or mathematics, Germany was a leader in the early 20th century. The majority of the country was moderate to liberal, and yet they just believed that, in the end, good manners would prevail. But that's not how it works. That's extreme naiveté. I would urge us to read history. That's all I would say. We don't need to have ideological arguments in this church. We should just talk about real stuff. Not, "I believe in this idea or that idea." Real stuff. Stuff that really happened to real people throughout real history.

It only takes a few committed people—along with the complacency of the masses—to allow atrocities to happen. And it's not even complacency. After all, there are a lot of people who are concerned, who are praying, who are truly disturbed by what is happening. But there's such a thing as wishful thinking, and wishful thinking is one of the most dangerous things we have to face now. Who doesn't want to hope for the best? Who doesn't want things to eventually work out? But that's just not how the real world works. As followers of Jesus Christ, we have to be as committed to resisting the evil that is emerging in our time, as are those who are working to further white supremacy.

The kind of Christian life that we're trying to live at [Church of All Nations] represents the faith that we have that God created all of us equally in God's image; that Jesus came to live and die and be raised again to show us true human dignity; and that we are to live together in harmony in the way that the whole universe was designed to be harmonious. All of that is at risk if we are naïve.

We must resist a fascist state. Is that a strange thing to say? Fascism is basically an ethno-nationalist belief that one group should dominate others by using raw power. That whoever claims the piece of land, the real estate, as their God-given, ethnic claim, that they have every right to use whatever means necessary, including military means, to claim it for themselves and exclude others from it.

If we think that niceness and politeness and wishful thinking is going to make all of this go away, then we clearly have not learned anything real or important from the history of Germany. Nor have we closely understood the history of our country, which from its inception subjugated people of color in the service of the interests of white people, whether it be the treatment of Native Americans or enslaved Africans. And these neofascists and neo-Nazis are trying to live into what has long been part of this country's history: that white people should gain all the spoils and run the country, and if there are nonwhite people here, they should serve the interests of white people. And if people of color stop providing free labor (or cheap labor at least), if they stop complying, if they start to resist oppression of any kind, then one has the right to wipe them out, in one way or another.

That's fascism, and that logic has been at work in this country before. It's kind of ebbed and flowed; there's been stronger times of oppression, and weaker times. If we don't look at the whole history, we might not understand the nature of our republic. But the racism is strong and it's deep and it's real.

This is the state our country is in now. We have some people who get the times we live in, who understand that we need to be aware, alert, and conscious (or, as they say, woke). And if we can't actually be a constructive part of moving our nation forward in a better direction, then, at the very least, we have to open our ears enough to get out of the way, so we don't inhibit the work of others. At the very least we must do no harm, which is the basic oath that doctors take before they practice medicine. We've got to stop bringing our fragility and ideology and abstract arguments into every little thing. Lives are in the balance here. We must listen. We must take seriously what people are saying, especially people of color. There is an immediate threat that some of us feel.

I do understand history and I'm sensing that something has shifted in our nation. Some holding wall has been breached; something has spilled over and it's not going to be easily fixed. It's going to take years, if not decades, to get us back to a different kind of social reality. While this kind of ugliness is always going be there in one form or another, something has been released in our nation that is seriously alarming to people of color and those in solidarity with them.

The highest love is loving one's enemy. That should be our north star, right? There's a lot of controversy right now about left-wing violence and right-wing violence.[2] I'm not interested in violence of any kind. I've been committed to nonviolence for many years. However, if someone were to physically attack my wife or children, I'm pretty sure that I would have an immediate physical response to that, even if that caused great physical harm to me. That's not violence as a response to violence. That is appropriate advocacy, in an appropriate context, if you truly are trying to protect the vulnerable. If someone is about to physically assault one of our little ones, I don't know what I would do in that moment, except to try to physically block it. This isn't an abstract argument about violence. It's, "How do we protect the most vulnerable in any way we can when the state is not protecting the vulnerable? When the police forces and the military are on the side of the racists?"

This is a dangerous time for our church family, too. No matter how progressive and radical our white members may be, the truth is that neofascists are not going to come for the white people, unless you stand in their way; they're going to come for people of color first. And there are white supremacist police departments all over the country that are just going to let it happen, as we've just seen in Charlottesville, and as we've seen in north Minneapolis . . . and as we've seen just about everywhere.

We could easily divide this congregation among those who are in physical danger and those who are not. And that would even split some of our marriages right down the line. We cannot do that. We're not going to let the sociology of our country impact and pervert our sociology of the church. We are all the same in God's sight; we are one. Skin color is the least important distinction in God's sight. Every single person here is beautiful in God's sight. One of the main reasons we started Church of All Nations was to say, "Can a group who believes in Jesus Christ overcome 500 years of racist legacy?" This is a historical church, because we're the product of history; we're trying to overcome the forces of history. We have these present historical forces pressing down upon us now. We have to remember why we're here. Every single one of us has to remember why we joined this church, and why we're still here. It's that important, right now, to remember.

These forces haven't gone away; they've actually been stoked by the current president, and unleashed in this world. There is a brazenness which I've never seen before; the brazenness of overt racism, neo-Nazism, fascism, that I have never seen in my 42 years of living in this country. I don't want to be alarmist, but we have to have these conversations. We can't be naïve.

Perhaps some of you have read the book *Night,* by Elie Wiesel. It includes a story about a Jewish man who somehow escapes a concentration camp and goes back to his hometown to warn his fellow villagers: "When they tell you to pack up and wear your best clothes, this is a trick. . . . When they tell you to get on that train, do not do it. Run for your lives right now."

But he was haggard. His clothes were falling apart. He was starving to death. He barely got to his home village. And they said, "This guy is crazy. This guy has gone mad." Nobody believed him, and they got on those trains and went to those concentration camps.[3]

We can't be naïve. We have to understand the true history and the true heart of what is going on. As a senior pastor, I'm not willing to stand before

God on Judgment Day and say that I led the congregation through wishful thinking, while my people were carted away.

Some ominous clouds are rolling in, and we need to be ready.

We are called to care for each other. We have to care about each other as we would care for people in our own nuclear family. We have to care as much about people who don't look like us, or have a similar background as us, as we care about those who do. And if we care for each other, and love each other as Jesus taught us, then we will know what to do when the time comes.

---

[1]The full sermon can be heard in its entirety at the Church of All Nations website, http://www.cando.org/sermons/overcome-evil-with-good/.

[2]Editor's note: This controversy became all the more prominent when it came to light that Antifa demonstrators were credited with saving some of the lives of those protesting the neo-Nazis in Charlottesville. See especially the comments made by Brandy Daniels and Cornel West in Dahlia Lithwick, "Yes, What about the 'Alt-Left'?" *Slate*, August 16, 2017, http://www.slate.com/articles/news_and_politics/politics/2017/08/what_the_alt_left_was_actually_doing_in_charlottesville.html.

[3]This is a paraphrased retelling inspired by a story in the book.

# 11

## The Sleepless Night:
## A Sermon on Ferguson, Keeping
## Awake, and Jesus

**Layton E. Williams**

In addition to being the audience engagement editor for Sojourners, Rev. Layton E. Williams is a writer who focuses on intersections of faith, justice, politics, and culture, with an emphasis on sexuality and gender. This sermon was preached at Fourth Presbyterian Church in Chicago on November 30, 2014, while she was serving as the pastoral resident at Fourth Presbyterian Church.

• • •

*Mark 13:24-37*

Last Monday night, a little after midnight, I was having a debate with myself. Should I go to sleep or stay awake? Like many of you, perhaps, I had spent my evening anxiously awaiting the decision from the grand jury on whether or not Officer Darren Wilson would be indicted for the killing of Mike Brown. I had spent hours refreshing news websites until the statement was finally released, and then when it became clear that Wilson would not be indicted or tried, I spent hours more following Ferguson Twitter feeds and reading countless Facebook posts as friends and public figures alike processed the news.

In Ferguson and in other cities around the country, including Chicago, protesters and those tasked with keeping the peace faced a long sleepless night. Undoubtedly, the family of Mike Brown faced the most sleepless night of all, following on the heels of many other sleepless nights in the weeks and months since his death.

Ensconced as I was on a tucked away South Carolina island with my family, I felt far removed from the unrest happening half a country away from me. But when the time came to turn off the lights and sleep and hope for a better tomorrow, I kept thinking of all those who weren't sleeping. And how for most of them, that sleeplessness *was* about the death of one young man and the one who killed him, but it was also about the seeming hopelessness of a deeply entrenched, insidious and deadly system of racism, classism, and injustice that continues to rent our society asunder even and especially when those of us with the privilege to do so simply turn out the light and sleep through it. And so, removed as I felt, sleeping seemed very much like the wrong thing to do.

Over and over, all night long, I thought about this text and what it means to "Beware, keep alert; for you do not know when the time will come" (Mk. 13:33).

This Sunday is the first Sunday of Advent, that season in our church life when we prepare our hearts and lives for the radical, world-transforming change that the birth of the Christ child will bring. Advent is a season of waiting and expectation, and each week we light candles and lean into that waiting with a spirit of hope, peace, joy, and love. This first week, we light the candle of hope, and this particular week, we could sure use some.

I confess that—much as I love the season leading up to Christmas—I have always found it a bit theologically confusing that we pretend to be waiting for a birth that has already happened several millennia ago. I always find myself thinking of the life and death that lie ahead for that baby in Bethlehem, and this year in particular I find myself thinking of his mother's anguish as she watched him on the cross and the rage and fear of his followers in the wake of his execution, and perhaps most of all—as I reflect on "keeping awake" in this oh so broken world—I think of that long night in the garden when Jesus trembled and prayed and begged his friends to stay awake with him.

It's true that we live in a time long after Christ was born, but these days it's not hard to imagine that we are still waiting. We still live in deep brokenness, and, indeed, we are still waiting for the radical transformation of the world that Christ promises. And we are still longing for "those days, after that suffering, [when] the sun shall be darkened, and the moon will not give its light . . . and [we] shall see the Son of Man coming" (Mk. 13:24–26). We are still waiting and we are still looking for hope in the ever-present darkness.

In the midst of that waiting and looking for hope, this passage calls us to be alert . . . wakeful . . . sleepless.

There is a particular moment in childhood when nothing seems quite so exciting as staying awake all night at a sleepover. I remember giggling my way through that slaphappy phase where exhaustion has made you feel delirious. I remember the strange sense of accomplishment that came with derailing our circadian rhythms so that, without sleep, a new day seemed to become an extension of the day before.

As adults, we learn to appreciate sleep. We live for naps. We come to fear the delirium and disorientation and disconnection from the world around us that exhaustion brings. We recognize that our bodies need time to rest and recover. We rejoice at the chance to go to sleep and wake to a better tomorrow.

But when it comes to our spiritual lives—maybe our childhood recklessness has some wisdom to offer. For we are told to keep alert, beware, and keep awake for we know not when the Son of Man will come.

In this passage, Jesus tells us that, "[T]his generation will not pass away until all these things have taken place" (Mk. 13:30). It certainly feels like a lot longer than that. We could easily conclude that this sentiment belongs to a more apocalyptic era than ours, that it has become irrelevant. But what if, instead, we chose to believe that the time, the day, that we really belong to is the day of Christ—that all that has come to pass since that birth in Bethlehem and that trembling moment in the garden when Jesus asked us to stay is just one long night?

What does it mean to stay spiritually awake to that day even as we wait and cry out for the day that is promised? To allow our spiritual rhythms to draw us back to Jesus even as they draw us forward to the world yet to come? What does it mean to seem delirious to this world—this world of brokenness and injustice, where young black men die and mothers weep and no one sleeps easy and we wonder what justice even looks like and if we've ever really known? What does it mean to be disoriented to that world and alive to the world of Christ?

There is a lullaby playing in this age. It sounds like the media and the powers and popular culture and it's attempting to lull us into sleep, into complacency, with gentle whispers that we are better, that difference is to be feared, that the status quo must be maintained, and that we should not ever rock the boat. Daily we struggle with the destructive "isms" of race, class, sex, ability and more that tuck us into our privilege and kiss us goodnight. Our discomfort shushes us, our fear calms our restless hearts, and our need for easy answers tells us, "Just go to sleep, you'll feel better in the morning."

But Jesus tells us to keep awake.

The truth is that many in this world are sleepless. The brokenness we all live in cuts them down day after day and keeps them up night after night. We can choose to turn out the light in the face of their sleeplessness and dream of the morning, but Jesus is not off waiting for the morning sun.

Jesus is with the sleepless. Jesus is weeping with the parents, and gasping with the dying sons, and trembling with those civil servants who do truly seek to serve and protect. Jesus is flipping tables with the outraged and terrified and holding up his hands and saying over and over and over, "Black lives matter." Jesus is with the sleepless because Jesus is sleepless too—at this whole broken system that his world is so ensnared in. Jesus is with the sleepless and Jesus calls us to be sleepless too. It's not enough just to be sleepless, but it's where Jesus calls us to begin. Keep awake.

This first week of Advent is about waiting for a better world and we *are* waiting. But it's also about hope. And I think it's difficult, in weeks like this one, to find hope. I'm reluctant to settle for a candy-coated version that—intentionally or inadvertently—diminishes the truly heinous characteristics of our modern world. In my life as a white, upper-middle-class Christian American, I've been taught that hope looks like kindness in the face of violence and friendship in adversity.

And there is some of that this week. There is that viral photo of the young black protester in Portland crying and hugging a cop. There are stories of protesters who protected businesses from looting even while they protested. There are the powerful words of Michael Brown's family telling others who share their grief and anger, "let's not just make noise, let's make a difference."

But I've also been listening to friends who grew up learning to fear systems that claimed to protect, who were taught young that *they* were feared and hated by the world for the color of their skin. They've been talking about how there is hope, too, in outrage that refuses to be silenced. There is hope in the breaking point. There is hope, essential Christ-like hope, in the angry voice that says, "We will not sleep, and we will not calm down, and we will be heard. Our lives matter."

Michelle Alexander, author of *The New Jim Crow* (which confronts racial injustice in our legal system), wrote a piece this week for *The New York Times* about talking to her young son in the hours before the Ferguson decision. She reveals that at first she lied to him and said that she expected a hopeful outcome, but then she told him the truth. And in the wake of his outrage, she reflected:

> My son is telling me now that the people in Ferguson should fight back. A minute ago, he was reminiscing about waving to Officer Friendly. Now he wants to riot.
>
> I tell him that sometimes I have those feelings too. But now I feel something greater. I am proud of the thousands of people of all colors who have taken to the streets in nonviolent protest, raising their voices with boldness and courage, capturing the attention and the imagination of the world. They're building a radical movement for justice, one that would make the freedom fighters who came before them sing from the heavens with joy.
>
> I tell my son, as well as my daughters, as we sit around the dinner table, stories of young activists organizing in Ferguson, some of them not much older than they are. I tell them about the hip-hop artist Tef Poe, who traveled with Michael Brown's parents to Geneva to testify before a United Nations subcommittee about police militarization and violence. I tell them about activists

like Phillip B. Agnew, Tory Russell, Brittany Ferrell and Alexis Templeton, who marched in the streets and endured tear gas while waving signs bearing three words: "Black Lives Matter."

I've met some of these activists, I say. They believe, like you do, that we should be able to live in a world where we trust the police and where all people and all children, no matter what their color or where they came from, are treated with dignity, care, compassion and concern. These courageous young people know the tools of war, violence and revenge will never build a nation of justice. They told me they're willing to risk their lives, if necessary, so that kids like you can live in a better world.

My son is stirring his mashed potatoes around on his plate. He looks up and says, "Right now, I'm just thinking I don't want anything like this ever to happen again."[1]

There is hope in a child who cannot help but be incensed at the idea of an unjust world. There is hope in those who risk their lives for the possibility of a better world, who refuse to go unheard even if they have to scream. And there is hope too in the holy discomfort, in the irrepressible outrage, in that nauseating feeling in our gut that keeps us up at night at the thought of Mike Brown, Eric Garner, Trayvon Martin, Tamir Rice, and so many more. There is hope in the sleeplessness. It is the hope of the coming Christ, who whispers while we wait through that long sleepless night, "Keep awake, keep alert, do not let this broken world lull you to sleep and dream of no better reality. Be sleepless. Keep awake and hope. With one another—and with me."

---

[1]Michelle Alexander, "Telling My Son about Ferguson," *The New York Times*, November 26, 2014, https://www.nytimes.com/2014/11/26/opinion/ferguson-telling-my-son-michelle-alexander.html.

# 12

## And God Hovered over the Face of the Deep: Transgressing the Gender Binary

**Robyn Henderson-Espinoza**

As an activist-scholar, Dr. Robyn Henderson-Espinoza is the director of public theology initiatives at Faith Matters Network in Nashville, Tennessee, and visiting scholar at Vanderbilt University Divinity School. They preached this sermon at Middle Collegiate Church in New York City on November 19, 2017, the day before the Transgender Day of Remembrance.

• • •

*Genesis 1*

Good morning, church. Thank you for showing up for a guest preacher! Thank you also to Middle Collegiate for sharing your pulpit with a transgender Latinx. And thank you to Dr. Jacqui [Lewis] for being a pastor's pastor and a theologian's theologian.

It's good to be with you all this morning, and it's good to be thinking alongside the work that's been happening here at Middle Collegiate. I've known Dr. Jacqui for several years and have always known her to be a pastor and theologian who listens deeply to the cries of the multitude. When we gathered for lunch a couple of months ago just down the street—in the heart of the East Village—and began talking about gender and my own understanding of myself as a nonbinary transgender person—and I was also wearing a t-shirt that said "They / Them"—she invited me to come and preach on moving beyond the binary.

This is important work. Nonbinary visibility has been, in [Pierre Teilhard] De Chardin's language, "the slow work of God." And, likewise, I don't want to speed past the important work of understanding the ways in which language is a hegemonic tool that has been used to fortify politics, policies, and theologies. One sermon can't do all the work, but it's churches like Middle Collegiate that are taking seriously the importance of things

76

like "moving beyond the binary" by inviting a nonbinary trans*gressive Latinx to preach!

Let me say that just occupying this space is a move beyond the binary; it's a fundamental transgression of what is recognizable and what has been intelligible in the pulpit. My body in this space, in this place, is a move to destabilize what has been recognizable in the pulpit, and my hope is that by occupying this pulpit I am able to help give birth to conditions of possibility for greater transgressions to materialize for those who are most impacted by multisystem oppressions, like that of trans women of color, gender variant folks, and our gender fluid siblings.

This is enough in many ways—that is, being here—but the energy that animates my vocation as a public theologian and pastor to many queer and trans people demands that I offer a chance for us all to step into a new imagination, a new cosmology, even, that just doesn't make room for trans folks and gender variant folks, but transgresses our normative theological imagination into an imagination that is rooted in the politics of radical difference, so that the spaces and places we construct are for all of us and not just some of us who are recognizable to the dominant structure. Part of that particular work is raising up nonbinary visibility as an important piece to reimagining our theological and pastoral work. The other piece of this work is the work of deep accompaniment for those who simply cannot unhinge from the logic of the norm. The work is both/and, and this work is holy work as we seek to be human with one another and as we seek to re-mem-ber ourselves, especially those of us whose embodiment is threatened by the logic of dominance and as a result is unable to flourish.

When I began preparing for this sermon, I first went to the lectionary, but the Baptist in me capitulated to the prophetic edge of the Spirit and what bubbled up for me was the Genesis passage that narrates creation. The first passage that I want to mention is Genesis 1:1–2. It's the first of at least two creation stories that we have in the Hebrew Bible, and is where I want to begin this conversation of transgressing the gender binary.

When God created the heavens and the earth, the earth was a formless void and darkness covered the face of the deep. Some translations suggest that God hovered over the face of the deep. I like both the imagery of darkness covering the face of the deep, and I also like the suggestion that God hovered over the face of the deep. In many ways, holding these two passages together is part of what Gloria Anzaldúa called "nepantla." It's the space in/between—neither/nor and both/and. *Nepantla* is the space of becoming and helps us lean into a nondual and nonbinary imagination.

The Hebrew in this passage is quite beautiful and speaks to the absence of any sort of binary. Do we ever think about the positivity of the negative, or what theologians called apophatic theology? How might we harness new contours of an imagination from the place of the "non" or the place of the negative? We often don't think of darkness as good; even Plato and the writer of the Gospel of John demonized darkness in favor of the language of light. How might we embrace the language of the writer of Genesis in "the earth being a formless void" and mobilize darkness and the face of the deep as part of the creative process that is trans inclusive and trans positive?

The Hebrew word is *tehom* and this term is prior to gender, prior to the discursive reality that language labels, and *tehom* is radically material. Can we even begin to imagine something prior to gender? Something that is non-gendered? Can we even imagine something prior to language?

I want you to try . . . When I say "blue," do you think of the sky, or do you think of a little boy? When I say "pink," do you think of the Mary Kay Cadillac, or do you think of a little girl? And, is a Mary Kay Cadillac not already a gendered assumption of what a right and respectable woman might want?

My point is this: to think of something, anything, as prior to gender is not how we are socialized. So, we must make little moves against destruction to reimagine how the story of the beginning and the stories of creation are prior to gender.

This Hebrew term and reality, *tehom*, lacks any sort of gender—the *tehom* is the essence of becoming and helps us transgress the binary frameworks whose logics continue to trap us in an imagination that is failing us all. *Tehom* is the primordial waters of creation. *Tehom* is before and after any sort of binary and is the technology of becoming that gives flesh and bone to our humanity, but because of the discursive strategies and colonizing tendencies of language, our bodily becoming is forced into a politics of recognition that therefore stabilizes both our gender and selfhood into binary categories and a binary logic.

Let's return to *tehom* for a moment and revel in the possibility of how the primordial waters might initiate new contours of understanding gender beyond the binary.

It is as if the creative process of becoming narrates the bodily becoming of humanity, but because of tradition and politics and other commitments around our religious and empire leading traditions, we end up with an imagination and language that reinforces heteropatriachal frameworks. The consequence of this is a religion and spirituality of empire that is, in my opinion, just bad theology.

The creative process of becoming is something that falls outside the language and logic of the binary. We need to remember that there have always been particular politics and commitments at play in the ways that scripture has been interpreted that snuffs out the Spirit of interpretation, and when we commit to allowing creation to be a creative process of becoming—really allow the story of creation to be one that is before and beyond any sort of hegemonic binary that demands recognition—we realize that this is a first order step in unhinging from any sort of logic that demands binary logic.

Do you hear me, church? We consent to the logic of the norm and the logic of the binary because we don't have an imagination for anything else. My academic partner, Dr. Nikki Young, told me several years ago that the best thing queers have on our side is our imagination. Imagination is the fuel that helps us resist the logic of the norm, and it is the energetic flows that allow us to lean into new contours of becoming.

Where are you with your commitment to having a robust imagination for radical difference? For something other than the logic of the norm? For trans liberation that unbinds us from a logic that contorts our bodies, mind, and soul into a recognizable and respectable gender binary?

Let me share a story with you and help tie up some loose ends here about imagination and socialization and our everyday practices.

"Are you a boy or a girl?" asked a young kid the other day, trying to figure out what pronouns I use. This kid couldn't hardly say "pronoun," but could ask "are you a boy or a girl?" In appreciation for the question, I replied, "I am neither, and I use they, them, their pronouns." I say to them the most honest truth about myself in response to their deep curiosity because to them, I was not recognizable. Despite how cute it is for kids to ask about pronouns (and, of course, we should continue asking pronouns and not assume based on how we think someone identifies), we should hold in tension the complexity of this question, "Are you a boy or a girl?" Let me mention that this question exposes a larger problem with how we even understand our cosmology and the ways that we socialize one another into the binary, even in our curiosity. (If you're curious about the use of the word "cosmology," I mean the study of the origin or evolution of what is—think back to the *tehom* and those primordial waters.)

Even our cosmic understanding has demanded the logic of the binary.

I don't fit in the cosmology that Christianity has been teaching, and neither do other trans folks who fall outside the recognizable binary. But, of course, I would say that our cosmology that animates the Christian faith is not trans inclusive and we need to do better!

We've all been forced to capitulate to the logic of the binary. We are all subject to the logic and language of the binary, so what do nonbinary folks do? What do gender fluid folks do? How do we transgress the logic of the gender binary? I think scripture gives us some clues!

As a lifelong Baptist, I always appeal to scripture, and the prophetic edge that is the Spirit has helped me see once again that the religion and faith of my childhood can help us re-mem-ber ourselves, especially trans folks.

Looking at the second account of creation in Genesis 2:6, the writer says that "a stream would rise from the earth, and water the whole face of the ground." Then, in the next verse, "the LORD God formed man from the dust of the ground, and breathed into his nostrils the breath of life; and the man became a living being."

In this passage, gender is imposed onto *a-dam*, the earth creature. The earth creature was formed out of dust from the ground. This is before and after the gender binary. Tradition and empire have forced these creation stories to be narrated through a logic of the binary. But let's remember that dust, like that of *tehom,* is part of what is primordial, part of what is before and after the logic of the norm out of which the binary emerges.

Skipping down to 2:21–22, the writer of Genesis says:

"So the LORD God caused a deep sleep to fall upon the man, and he slept; then he took one of his ribs and closed up its place with flesh. And the rib that the LORD God had taken from the man he made into a woman and brought her to the man." We need to remember that the Hebrew gives us some clues. *A-dam* means "earth creature" and the English word, woman, is inserted here and is ascribed particular value throughout religious traditions, but we need to remember that the Hebrew indicates that Eve is from the earth, too. The creation of Eve is from Adam's rib— from the earth—from the non-place that is always and forever becoming.

God split Adam apart so the question we all should be asking is, "Was Adam both?" Or is Adam a nonbinary creature in the image of God (who is also nonbinary)? This is leaning into a new cosmic reality, a new cosmology, and a new theology that helps us learn how to be human with one another.

When we begin to think about humanity outside the coloniality of the gender binary, we not only destabilize the production of gendered knowledge, because as we all know our knowledge is highly gendered, but when we destabilize the production of gendered knowledge, our imagination expands into something that transgresses the gender binary.

Returning to the issue of cosmology and imagining a cosmology that is trans inclusive and trans positive means that we have an ontology and epistemology and ethics that is aligned with being trans inclusive and trans positive (these philosophical domains always impact theology!). And, so, if cosmology is the question of origin, so is ontology, which for our purposes is to more fully understand the question of being and becoming, which creates conditions for the production of knowledge to be more than what can be contained in the logic of the binary. The production of knowledge is often called epistemology, and you better believe that theologians have looked to philosophers to substantiate a production of knowledge that animates and fortifies cis-supremacy. Likewise, when we are able to imagine new contours of being and becoming and knowledge production, this helps us have new social practices, or ethics. All of this is work that has to be done to transgress the gender binary and the logic that holds the binary to the center of the Judeo-Christian cosmology. What we learn is that the center cannot hold the logic of the norm; the center is animated by the *tehom* and we must commit ourselves to the everyday practice of eradicating symbolic knowledge, language, social practices that reify a cosmology and creation story that only two genders are legitimate or recognizable.

And, if all of this is not enough, let me get super real with us all today about the reality of how our theologies of dominance are killing trans people and how little moves of destructiveness and moving beyond the binary might actually save lives.

As of this week, there have been 25 trans people murdered that we know of this year. This is the highest number of folks we have lost—kinfolk who have been stolen from us. Most of these kinfolk who have been murdered were trans women of color, and the murders of trans women of color is disproportionate to that of our other kin.

What does this mean? It means that our imagination of what is human is framed by the logic of the binary that also demands assimilating into the dominant structure of gender and, at times, race. Being trans does not mean you must assimilate into one of the binary categories, nor does it also mean you must assimilate in the dominant structure of race and power—read, you don't have to mimic whiteness. Our work today, the day before the Trans Day of Remembrance, is to lean into what *nepantla* is holding—the *tehom,* which is the vibrant energetic flows of becoming that mobilize us into an imagination of radical difference, so that our symbolic language, our social practices, and our ideas are not static and stabilized into a logic of the binary, but instead are animated by the energetic flows of the primordial waters—by the *tehom*—whose essence of becoming fortify our social practices as we learn to be human with one another outside a normative frame that demands a recognizable two-gender system.

Our work today is to hold one another in our deep complexity and in our deep unknowing as we lean into new contours of becoming different in the world and different to ourselves. The work of transgressing gender is in part transgressing our own imagination that tells us we cannot imagine or that tells us that we are failing to imagine. Our work today is to also remember our trans siblings who were stolen from us because of the lies of the logic of the gender binary.

May we commit to turning inward as much as we turn outward, so that our interior life and who we understand ourselves to be is deeply aligned with our social practices. May we transgress the logic of the norm and may we lean into the work that is remembering to imagine and remembering those who can no longer imagine with us.

Our work remains unfinished until all of us are free from the logic that keeps us trapped and categorized in ways that are only recognizable to the dominant sector. May those who are most impacted by the logic of the binary find freedom and liberation in knowing their own truth and the truth that God, too, animates a nonbinary visibility.

# 13

# Religion That Kills: A Sermon in Response to the Pulse Massacre

**Emily Bowen-Marler**

Rev. Emily Bowen-Marler is a pastor at Brentwood Christian Church (Disciples of Christ) in Springfield, Missouri, and the award-winning coauthor of *Toward a Hopeful Future.* This sermon was preached at Brentwood Christian Church on June 19, 2016, the week after the tragic shooting at Pulse nightclub in Orlando, Florida.

• • •

*Amos 5:21–24*

Last week, I stood before you during our time of prayer shaking as I shared the updated news that there were not 20 people killed at Pulse nightclub in the wee hours of Sunday morning as originally reported, but 49 people.

Forty-nine people killed by a hate-filled man wielding a semi-automatic rifle. He proclaimed allegiance to ISIS right before the attack, but he was an American citizen, born in New York and living in Florida.

This has been a hard week to get any work done. I spent a great deal of time pouring over my newsfeed, reading the reflections of my friends and family in the LGBTQ+ community, listening to their anguish and fear and desperate attempts to choose love in the face of such hatred, reaching out when I could, sharing messages of love and comfort. There were pleas from some to not use this massacre to pit two marginalized groups in our country—the LGBTQ+ community and the Muslim community—against one another. I read stories of solidarity between these two groups. In one community, a gay minister shared that the first clergy to reach out to him in the wake of the Orlando shooting was the Imam from the local mosque. I learned that in Tulsa, there is a history of the LGBTQ+ and Muslim communities showing up for one another whenever one or the other group is the target of hate. I read speeches by some who confessed their former poor treatment of gay people and then publicly apologized for that bad behavior. It's been a galvanizing week as I've seen allies all over the country speak out or sing out their solidarity and love for the LGBTQ+ community.

When religious violence takes place, a common knee-jerk reaction in our country is to blame Muslims. Aside from the fact that—since the September 11 attacks—white Christian nationalist groups are more responsible for religious violence than any other group in the United States, and the vast majority of Muslims around the world condemn ISIS (more Muslims are killed by ISIS than any other religious group), it's also important to point out that the deadly consequences of religious violence don't always come through the barrel of a gun.

Lest we give in to the temptation to lay all of the blame at the feet of the distorted version of Islam practiced by the shooter, let me remind you that we live in a city where it was *Christian* communities of faith that bolstered the repeal of the nondiscrimination ordinance in April of 2015, removing protections for those in the LGBTQ+ community as far as employment, housing, and public services are concerned. We live in a country where the response to the Supreme Court decision in favor of marriage equality last June has been a rash of hysterical anti-LGBTQ+ bills. And that's not an exaggeration; there have been over one hundred anti-LGBTQ+ bills debated in states across the country this year. As a friend's Facebook post pointed out:

> You say, "How could this tragedy happen?" It happened because [the shooter's] hate was born and bred in America, not overseas. Just two weeks ago you were calling trans women child predators. One year ago you were saying that our marriages should not be recognized. Six years ago you were saying that gay men and women couldn't die for their country. Ten years ago you told us we didn't deserve job protections. Thirteen years ago it took Lawrence v. Texas to decriminalize our sex lives. Eighteen years ago you took Matthew Sheppard. Twenty-three years ago you took Brandon Teena. Thirty-six years ago the American Government began their five years of silence as ten thousand gay men were massacred by the AIDS virus. Forty-three years ago we were still considered mentally ill. And forty-seven years ago the riots of Stonewall began. For centuries this country has bred homophobia into our history, in our schools, and into the very fabric of society. [The shooter] was the product of American hate . . . America, you taught him this and even sold him the gun to do it.[1]

Islam does not have the monopoly on anti-LGBTQ+ sentiments and behavior and it's time for America to look in the mirror and see the ways it has contributed to tragedies like the one that took place last Sunday. In fact, more Muslims in America support equal rights for LGBTQ+ persons than evangelical Christians do.[2]

I was listening to a podcast last week and those on the panel were discussing the shooting and the fact that the shooter was Muslim. One person said that fundamentalist Christians may stand on the streets with hate-filled signs to protest against and spew hatred toward the LGBTQ+ community, but it's only Muslims who would perpetrate a violent act like the Orlando shooting against those they abhor.

But I'm here to tell you that while there may not be cases of fundamentalist Christians entering gay nightclubs with semi-automatic rifles to kill and maim innocent people, the hateful rhetoric spewed forth from their mouths and from their pulpits toward members of the LGBTQ+ community has taken many more lives than were taken at Pulse last Sunday morning. Those sermons of hate, words of judgement, and damnation from a God who they claim loathes a certain segment of our society have placed guns in the hands of untold members of the LGBTQ+ community and all but pulled the trigger, taking precious lives through suicide. Don't tell me that the anti-LGBTQ+ rhetoric of fundamentalist Christianity doesn't kill, *it does*!

A friend of mine wrote a post earlier this week trying to explain to her cisgender straight friends and family the reality of being a gay woman in the United States of America:

> Here's the thing you need to understand about every LGBT person in your life. We've spent most of our lives being aware that we are at risk.

> When LGBT folks say "It could have been here. It could have been me," they aren't exaggerating. I don't care how long you've been out or how far down your road to self-acceptance and love you've traveled, all of us are always aware that we are at some level of risk.

> When I reach to hold my wife's hand in the car, I still do the mental calculation of "ok, that car is just slightly behind us so they can't see, but that truck to my left can see right inside the car." If I even think about kissing her in public, I'm never fully in the moment. I'm always parsing who is around us and paying attention to us. There's a tension that comes with that . . . a literal tensing of the muscles that brace me for potential danger. For a lot of us, it's become such an automatic reaction that we don't even think about it directly any more. We just do it . . .

> Over the last few years, it started to fade a little. It started to feel like maybe things were getting better. A string of Supreme Court decisions. Public opinion shifting to the side of LGBT rights. Life was getting better. You could breathe a little.

> I've had some time to adjust to the idea that people hate us enough to kill us. Matthew Shephard was my first real lesson in

that. So this weekend was a sudden slap in the face, a reminder that I should never have let my guard down, should never have gotten complacent... because it could have been me, my wife, my friends.

Every LGBT person you know, knows what I'm talking about. Those tiny little mental calculations we do over the course of our life add up . . . and this past weekend hit us with a stark reminder that those simmering concerns, those fears . . . they probably won't ever go away.

Additionally, now we just got a lesson that expressing our love could result in the deaths of *others* completely unrelated to us. It's easy to take risks when it's just you and you've made that choice. Now there's this subtext that you could set off someone who kills other people who weren't even involved. And that's a lot.

But we will be doing those mental calculations for the rest of our lives. Those little PDAs you take for granted with your spouse. They come with huge baggage for us.

So do me a favor. Reach out to that LGBT person you know and let them know you are thinking of them and you love them. That will mean the world to them right now. I promise.[3]

As I reflect on the grave ways the LGBTQ+ community has been harmed in the name of faith, in the name of Christianity, I feel shame for these practices of bad religion. It is tempting to turn one's back on faith when so much damage has been done in its name. But instead, I hold on to the very best aspects of faith, the teachings of love and inclusion shown by Jesus Christ, as well as the prophetic voices crying out in Hebrew scripture— voices like Isaiah, Jeremiah, and Amos. Voices that shed a light on the injustices in their world and proclaimed a different way in the name of God. Good religion does not stay silent in the face of injustice and hatred.

I was fortunate enough to grow up in an open and affirming congregation. I had two gay youth group leaders; I have lifelong friends who are gay. I do what I can to speak and act in love and support for the LGBTQ+ community. But something in my friend's post galvanized me to do something more. With it being Pride week, I wanted to do something special to declare my love and support in a way that would be clear to all. So I made a sign. A sign inspired by the Benediction we say at the end of every Sunday morning worship service here at Brentwood Christian Church. And I thought it was important for everyone to know that I'm saying this as a clergy person, someone raised in the church, someone following the way of Jesus, someone trained in the Bible and theology. So I made a sign that said, "As a pastor, I want you to know that you are

LOVED beyond your wildest imagination JUST AS YOU ARE." My sign had bold letters and bright colors, because I've been to Pridefest other years and I've seen signs of hate held up with bold letters that demeaned the LGBTQ+ community. I held up my sign as I walked in the Equality March yesterday morning. And then I set it up at the Brentwood booth for all who walked by to see. One woman stopped by with her wife to color an affirmation card we had on the table. After she finished coloring, she said, "I have to tell you. Thank you for saying this, for showing us that the church can have a message of love for us. Because too often all we've heard is a message of hate and rejection." She started to cry as she told me of how the church she and her wife attended (the church her wife grew up in) had kicked them out of the ministry they were an integral part of, and how, after that, they had also been asked to leave the church. How one of the women in the church tried to give them a hug as she said, "We only say these things out of love." She and I hugged and cried. Person after person came to our booth, telling us how happy they were to see a message of love and welcome coming from a church. As the day went by, total strangers came up to me, hugging me, some with huge smiles, some with tears in their eyes, some with wavering voices, as they thanked me for standing up in love, as they told me stories of how their churches had rejected them or their loved ones. It was incredible, the need for people to hear that message of love. Especially in the wake of Orlando, when their illusions of security were shattered with gunfire and their fears were ripped wide open.

If we are to practice religion that gives life, rather than takes it, we must not stay silent in the face of hate. We must not stay silent in the towering shadows of those who might try to bully us into keeping our mouths shut. We must not stay silent when people respond, "Now, let's not get political!" For too long, we've allowed the accusation that we're venturing into the territory of politics to keep us quiet. It's time we realize that the politicization of every issue that actually matters was done on purpose to divide and conquer, to silence the masses and stymie change.

We must not stay silent in the barrage of attacks on the transgender community through bathroom legislation. We must not stay silent when 49 people are killed and 53 injured in a mass shooting at a gay nightclub. We must not stay silent when it seems that a person's right to own a semi-automatic rifle is more important than another person's right to dance with their friends without fear of being gunned down. The time for silence is over. We've held vigils and those were necessary. We need time to mourn, time to grieve the devastating loss of life. But these deaths must not end in our silence. It's time our nation woke up to this culture of hate for the LGBTQ+ community that has been bred for far too long.

Our scripture reading for this morning is one I go back to time and time again when I wrestle with issues of injustice in our world. The prophet Amos says to us:

I hate, I despise your festivals,

and I take no delight in your solemn assemblies.
Even though you offer me your burnt-offerings and
grain-offerings,

I will not accept them;
and the offerings of well-being of your fatted animals

I will not look upon.
Take away from me the noise of your songs;

I will not listen to the melody of your harps.
But let justice roll down like waters,

and righteousness like an ever-flowing stream.

In the face of injustice, Amos cried out. In the wake of exploitation of the poor, Amos was not silent. Amos decried the solemn assemblies where people offered prayers and burned offerings, because he saw that nothing ever changed. He saw that their action ended with their prayers, rather than began with them. Theologian Karl Barth got it right when he said, "To clasp the hands in prayer is the beginning of an uprising against the disorder of the world."

May we go from our candlelight vigils as people changed. May we go from our moments of silence as people transformed. May we go from our houses of worship with our mighty voices raised proclaiming a message of hope and love for all of God's people. Voices raised proclaiming an end to hate and fear and war. Voices raised celebrating the dignity and worth of every human being. With our voices raised, we can begin to see justice roll down like waters and righteousness like an ever-flowing stream. Thanks be to God.

---

[1]Sarah Slone, "The Roots of the Anti-LGBTQ Massacre in Orlando," *Liberation*, June 18, 2016, https://www.liberationnews.org/the-roots-of-the-anti-lgbtq-massacre-in-orlando/.

[2]See the statistics available at the Pew Research Center, http://www.pewforum.org/2017/07/26/political-and-social-views/pf_2017-06-26_muslimamericans-04new-06/.

[3]Private Facebook correspondence shared only with friends.

# 14

# When Our Thoughts and Prayers Turn to Ash: Religion, Gun Violence, and America

**Aric Clark**

Rev. Aric Clark is a writer, speaker, and Presbyterian minister who currently serves a two-point Methodist charge in the Portland area. He is the coauthor of *Never Pray Again: Lift Your Head, Unfold Your Hands, and Get to Work,* and pastor at Sherwood United Methodist Church in Sherwood, Oregon. He preached this sermon at Sherwood on Ash Wednesday, February 14, 2018, just hours after yet another tragic school shooting in the United States, this time at Marjory Stoneman Douglas High School in Parkland, Florida.

• • •

*Psalm 137; Isaiah 58:1–12*

Excuse me for starting this with a whisper. I want you to know, before the shouting begins, why it is necessary. I want you to feel the need to scream from your center down to the soles of your feet and out to the tips of your fingers. Because this is a prayer that we have to get into our bodies, into our skin and bones, if we are to have any hope of carrying it into the world.

This afternoon at least 17 people, 14 of them children, were murdered by a gunman at Marjory Stoneman Douglas High School in Parkland, Florida. Fourteen children who said goodbye to their parents in the morning, went to school, and who will never come home. They died in their classrooms, surrounded by their peers and teachers, huddling in fear for their lives.

In any other time and place but now in America that news would surely produce spontaneous shouts of grief and lamentation, but in us it hardly even provokes surprise. It could be relegated to the scrolling text of a banner at the bottom of our television screen, or rapidly pass by our eyes as we scan our social media feed and it might not significantly alter our mood. We have arrived at a place of spiritual emptiness: of desolation. We neither hope nor despair. The blood of children stains desks and chalkboards and it pains us little.

I hope you will agree with me that this is a sign of grave spiritual disease. We must urgently recover our capacity to mourn, we must figure out how to scream again, before death destroys even the memory of meaning in our lifetime.

"Shout!" God instructed the prophet Isaiah, "Shout out and do not hold back!" Isaiah, who was friend to kings and familiar with the temple courtyards, was instructed to shout in these spaces accustomed to gentility, accustomed to reserve, and manners, and respectful debate. Shout, god damn it! For the workers oppressed in the fields who grew this grain you just laid on the altar, and who raised those calves being led in for the sacrifice. Shout for the enslaved, for the indebted, for the widowed, and the orphaned. Shout like a trumpet that while we ignore injustice in our midst our religion is empty; our thoughts and our prayers are pointless wind.

Indeed, it is our thoughts and prayers that have taken the wind out of our screams, which should be echoing through our cities. We have thought and prayed our way into this mess. As the predictable stream of thoughts and prayers pour out from our politicians on Twitter it takes us only a click to discover how much money they have received from the National Rifle Association to fund those thoughts and those prayers. Like the reveal at the end of a *Twilight Zone* episode it becomes suddenly clear that the God we've all been praying to is not the God revealed in Jesus of Nazareth, but Moloch, and the dying children are sacrifices, and the gun smoke rising is like incense from the altar. Someone's prayers at least have been heard and answered.

The perverse religiosity of contemporary America understands violence not as an evil to be prevented, or even as a grim option of last resort, but as the foundation of a hellish freedom, where every individual is only free to the degree they are able to destroy their neighbor. It increasingly appears to me that we've moved beyond even myths of redemptive violence wherein the selective retributive violence enacted against a few sustains the possibility of community for the majority. Now we embrace a violence that is not just arbitrary, but also random, and employ it tautologically as the justification for continually increasing our collective capacity to destroy everything and everyone.

I am sure that you, like me, are exhausted from arguing about guns, so do not mistake this sermon as another list of arguments. Arriving as we have at this juncture of near total epistemic closure, of ideologies elevated to dogma, and complete spiritual collapse our response cannot be debate. We have to somehow roll the stones away from the tombs. We have to stomp and shake the ground until the graves break open. We have to scream until the dead rise.

This is why the liturgy of Black Lives Matter is more powerful than the liturgy of the church these days. Because when we are in the streets shouting "Say His Name" and the names of the dead children: Trayvon Martin, Mike Brown, Christopher Kalonji, Quanice Hayes, Tamir Rice, and so many others ring from our collective voices so loud that we feel them vibrating off our skin, echoing in our bones; and when we've been saying their names for so long that our voices are growing hoarse, then our bodies become the prayer. My hoarse, pained throat is the manifest absence of the loved ones stolen from us by violence. Your ringing ears are the echo of their life from beyond the grave.

But today is Ash Wednesday, and it is an opportunity for us to recover the vitality of our faith. In Lent our prayers get real. They get dirty. Our prayers become ash on our foreheads mingling with our sweat and running into our eyes. Our prayers become hunger in our bellies, pleasures and distractions set aside not from a misguided effort at self-punishment, but due to the certain conviction that unless we somehow work this spiritual agony out in the flesh we will continue our servitude to death. Unless we become living prayers committed to breaking the yoke of Moloch in our culture then all of our worship is a dead end.

So come. Come feel the grit of these dead palms, and the oil of the pressed olives on your skin. Come remember how fragile, how temporary, and how precious your ordinary human life is to God. Let us learn together how to shout again, and how to sing by rivers in Babylon when tears for our dead babies choke our hearts. Let us raise our voices until they cannot be ignored, until we can be heard over the report of bullets, over the ring of profits, over the mindless recitation of another round of thoughts and prayers. And let our message be, "enough!"

# 15

# Encountering Pharaoh—and Climate Change

**Leah D. Schade**

Rev. Dr. Leah D. Schade is the assistant professor of preaching and worship at Lexington Theological Seminary in Kentucky and the author of *Creation-Crisis Preaching: Ecology, Theology, and the Pulpit.* While this sermon was originally preached in 2015 at United in Christ Lutheran Church in Lewisburg, Pennsylvania, its reflections on climate change make it as timely as ever. It's also included in this volume as a reminder that powerful forces of oppression and destruction aren't limited to one particular political figure or time, but are with us in myriad ways over many eras.[1]

• • •

*Exodus 7:1-7; 8:1-15*

How did they get themselves into this mess? Frogs everywhere! In their sinks, in their shoes, in their pots and in their pews!

One frog hopping is a source of delight. Hundreds of frogs keep you awake all night!

Where did this mess come from? And what are they going to do about it? Everyone is looking to Pharaoh, the mighty ruler of Egypt, to wield his divine power and rid the land of these ambitious amphibians. But they're beginning to suspect that maybe Pharaoh isn't as powerful as the propaganda says he is. If he can't even control a simple thing like frogs, maybe they need to reconsider who's really in charge here.

While the people might be thinking that, Pharaoh certainly was not. Pharaoh relied on himself and his own power. That power was very real, and it was symbolized by the panoply of gods and goddesses that were believed to control all aspects of Egyptian life. The goddess of the Nile, for example, controlled the river that was the lifeblood of the valley. But since

Pharaoh controlled the priests who consorted with the river goddess, he believed that *he* controlled the water.

Similarly, the goddess of birth had a symbol, too. It was a frog. Since Pharaoh controlled the priests who consorted with that goddess, he also believed he controlled the fertility of his people.

And on it went. This assumption that Pharaoh controlled the supernatural spectrum extended to all aspects of life and creation. Pharaoh controlled the crops and harvest. Pharaoh controlled the livestock. Pharaoh controlled people's health. Pharaoh controlled their children. Pharaoh even believed he controlled the light of the sun itself. But worst of all, he believed he controlled the very forces of life and death. It did not matter to him that this belief resulted in suffering when God disrupted his cruel reign. What mattered was securing his own position, wealth, and power at all costs.

Does any of this sound familiar in our own time? We, too, have leaders who believe they control the world's resources and wealth. They have almost god-like power. The rulers of global corporations, governments, and elite financial centers are the Pharaohs of our time who believe they are answerable to no one. They serve the god of profit, commodifying every aspect of the earth and people's labor.

"Who am I to go to Pharaoh?" Moses asked when God called him to confront the supreme leader in order to free the Israelites. "What is one person in the face of these awesome powers? What difference can I possibly make? Pharaoh is too big—too big to fail—and I am nothing but a peon. It will make absolutely no difference whether I act or not."

God begs to differ. Because there is nothing that irritates God more than someone who thinks he's god. Whether it's people or organizations, corporations or governments—when they control so much and can act with such impunity, this really gets under God's skin. So God sends Moses and Aaron to bring a message to Pharaoh: let my people go to worship the true God. Because you are not god, Pharaoh. You only think you are. And if you do not humble yourself before the true God, there will be dire consequences for you and all those who support your reign.

Pharaoh, of course, responded the way most people in power do when they are confronted. He hardened his heart. *Kavad-lev* is the word in Hebrew. Whether it was by God's action or his own, the result was the same. Pharaoh's heart was made impermeable and impenetrable with his own riches and glory. He made himself dense with his own sense of omnipotence. His heart became insensitive. He could not feel.

So God had to bring down every one of Pharaoh's illusions of power in order to break through to his heart. God sent plague after plague to reveal the impotence of Egypt's gods, and, by extension, Pharaoh himself. The river was turned to blood until Pharaoh promised to let the people go. But then he went back on his word when Moses returned the water to its previous state of cleanness. Frogs filled his palace and the homes of all his people, and then lay dying and stinking in the hot sun. It became apparent that Pharaoh really had no power over birth or any other part of creation. Flies. Gnats. Boils on the skin. Locusts. Severe weather events that destroy crops. Strange diseases that kill livestock. Every one of those plagues meant another false god crumbled, along with Pharaoh's own power. He was given multiple chances to humble himself and recognize that his place was to serve his people, and to serve God's creation, not to dominate them and use them for his own profit. But never once did he release his grip on his power or his people. So when God finally brings him all the way down to his knees, cradling his dead son, Pharaoh drags an entire nation down with him. It is a devastating reckoning.

When I look around at our world today and see the devastation brought on by global climate disruption, I wonder if we are witnessing another devastating reckoning of biblical proportions. The plagues are upon us. Invasive species. Alternating floods and droughts. Severe weather events. Decimated crops. Strange diseases in our fish and livestock, as well as our own bodies.

Are there messages in these plagues that we are not heeding? Are those of us who have enjoyed decades of privilege hardening our hearts to the suffering of those most vulnerable just so we can enjoy the lifestyle of a rich Pharaoh? Are we worshiping gods that are illusions? Are we being given opportunities to humble ourselves and recognize that our place is to serve each other and to serve God's creation, rather than dominate them and use them for our own profit? And are we in danger of bringing down an entire planet by not releasing our grip of privilege and dominance?

Perhaps we shouldn't be too hard on Pharaoh. Maybe it wasn't just blind stubbornness that encased his heart with stone-cold steel. Maybe it was plain, old-fashioned fear. He knew that if he released the Israelites, his country would lose its energy source, and he would lose the source of his god-like control. The Israelite slaves were what fueled the Egyptian economy. Freeing the Hebrews would have meant disruption, change, and the loss of free labor that enabled their incredible wealth and comfort. But that wealth came at the expense of incredible suffering.

However, it was more than just wealth. Allowing the Israelites their freedom to worship God would have meant Pharaoh and the Egyptians would lose their sovereignty. Their dominion was dependent on the subjugation of the Israelites. They refused to see that at the core of their identity and their national pride was the humiliation and deaths of countless people.

Maybe on some level, Pharaoh and the Egyptians knew that if they let themselves truly see the suffering of the people they enslaved, they would be overcome by guilt and grief. Those are feelings no one wants to experience. So Pharaoh and the Egyptians tightened their grip and hardened their hearts, defying the commands of God.

Maybe the hardening of hearts we see today is also driven by plain, old-fashioned fear. If we release our grip on fossil fuels, we will lose our energy source. That's a scary prospect. But there is a cost to this seemingly cheap energy that is too high to pay. The pollution of air, water, and land. The cancers and other health issues of those who live in the "sacrifice zones" of the industry. The melting of glaciers and flooding of island nations and coastlands as the atmosphere warms from $CO_2$ trapping the sun's heat. Yes, the transition to renewable energy means radical change. But there are healthier ways to power our economy that do not lead to a climate breakdown and ecological sepsis. No amount of wealth and comfort is worth this kind of suffering.

But it's more than just wealth. Many people worry that if we agree to international climate accords, the United States will lose its sovereignty. Yet the reality is that our dominion is dependent on the subjugation of the entire planet. We are refusing to see that at the core of our identity and national pride is the humiliation and death of humans and earth-kin alike.

Maybe on some level, our leaders and we ourselves know that if we truly see the suffering of people enslaved to our fossil fuel addiction, we will be overcome by guilt and grief. And that can be paralyzing. So we tell ourselves—better to hold on to what we've worked so hard to build. Better to tighten the grip, harden our hearts, and dig in our heels. Even if it means defying the commands of God.

But here's the thing: God has already made the decision that injustice can no longer rule. Trying to grasp the old ways only leaves us with clenched fists and hardened hearts. The enslavement of earth and human beings is no longer the way we can fuel our economy. What worked before isn't working now. And, truth be told, it never worked that well to begin with. Because look at the mess it's gotten us into. Relying on the Fossil Fuel Pharaohs brings us nothing but disease, catastrophes, and death.

So the question for us is this: Will we continue to harden our hearts and clench our fists? Or will we loosen our grip, open our hearts, and trust that God has something else in store for us?

It's time to turn the plague of *frogs* into the acronym F.R.O.G.: Fully Rely On God. It's time to soften our hearts, open our hands, and give ourselves over to the task of making the just transition to an economy powered by sun, wind, waves, and geothermal energy. It's time to let go of our excuses and stop rationalizing our self-serving reasons for hardening our hearts.

It wouldn't have been so bad if Pharaoh's decisions only affected himself. But what he failed or refused to realize is that his stubbornness would be the downfall of his people. When the stoniness of his heart finally cracked, the pieces fell and crushed everyone around him, including his own beloved son. Just as he ordered the children of the Hebrews to be murdered, he would now watch his own son die in his arms from a plague of his own making.

And that is the real tragedy, isn't it? When the ones in charge, the ones with power, influence, and resources make the decision not to care, not to act, not to respond to God's command, it is ultimately the children who suffer. The children of Egypt suffered from the plagues because the adults refused to respond to God's commands.

So it is today, and so it could be far into the future if we do not learn the lessons of Egypt. The ones in charge, the ones with power, influence, and resources have made the decision not to care, not to act, not to respond to God's command to live in right relationship with earth. They have hardened their hearts. They may believe they have every right and reason to do so. But who ends up suffering in the end? The children. This is what is breaking *my* heart. I fear that we are giving up on our own children and their future.

But I also know this: the children of earth are not giving up on us. They are rising up in court rooms and classrooms, on Native reservations and at international conferences. They are calling us to account. Like Moses sent from the burning bush, they are demanding that we release them from the chains of fossil fuels. God's voice speaks through them—let my children go! Release them to live in a world with clean water and air, with forests and healthy ecosystems, with birds and animals who have enough room to live and grow and thrive. They are demanding that we take care of this earth and rebuild the foundations of our economy and energy. They are calling on us to clean up and restore the systems they need to survive—the health system, the education system, the food system. And they are *fully relying on God* to lead them into a promised land. It's time to join them and discover just how powerful our God really is.

---

[1]Editor's note: On the Sunday of this sermon, the congregation brought frogs to church—toy frogs, plush frogs, frog decorations and posters, and even live frogs in containers. So the entire sanctuary was filled with frogs!

# 16

# Hope for All the Earth: A Sermon from Standing Rock

**David Swinton**

Rev. Dr. David Swinton is the senior minister of Grace United Methodist Church in Des Moines, Iowa. He received his MDiv from Garrett-Evangelical Seminary and DMin from McCormick Theological Seminary. This sermon was preached at Grace on November 27, 2016, just after his return from the Standing Rock Reservation in the Dakotas.

• • •

*Psalm 122*

Last week I traveled up to the Standing Rock Reservation where Native people and supporters are protesting an oil pipeline across the Missouri River. I wanted to see what was going on, to bring some donations from our church, and to support the Native people there. But actually participating in the protests? I wasn't sure.

I have personal guidelines about participation in protests. I think that protests need to (1) directly pressure the people who make decisions, (2) have a clear message about the desired result, and (3) make sure the action highlights the bad behavior of others, not those protesting. Aside from a couple of harmless peace marches, these guidelines have allowed me to squirm out of every single protest action that has come along.

It's not really about my high standards. Personal reasons overshadow them. It's because I don't like feeling people's disapproval (let alone their anger). I don't like any kind of chaos (even the crowd at the state fair and the farmer's market is too much for me). And I'm used to being in charge (even though when I'm in charge I complain about it constantly).

No, when it comes to making a statement, or taking a stand, I would much rather write letters from the comfort of my own home—more in sorrow, than in anger. But last week, my curiosity surpassed my timidity.

My old friend, Rob Patton—minister-turned-livestock farmer—talked me into going on a trip to Standing Rock in North Dakota.

I confess that I was moved to go, not necessarily because I had strong feelings about the pipeline, but by compassion for those who do. Also, I wanted to spend some time with Rob

and I had never been to North Dakota before and knew I was *never* going to take a vacation there.

So on Thursday, November 17, we set off with donations of food, blankets, money, and indoor propane heaters. I also took my tool box and a couple stoles for us to wear in case we took part in the demonstrations. And if by chance we joined a protest that was sprayed by tear gas, I wanted to be prepared [dons mask and goggles].

We arrived on Friday and found places to unload our various donations. On Saturday we attended a long orientation with about 120 other newcomers. We began and closed with prayer and Native song. We learned the seven values of the Lakota people: Prayer, Respect, Compassion, Honesty, Generosity, Humility, and Wisdom.

We were asked to consider everything we do—every meeting, every meal, even our movement around the camp—with a sense of ceremony. We were asked to observe camp protocols: no weapons, alcohol, or drugs allowed. And to please refrain from cursing. (The ban on cursing makes it hard for me to fully express how cold it was up there.) But we were well prepared with many layers of clothing, and a travel trailer. We were the fortunate ones. Most people were in teepees and tents.

On Saturday afternoon, as Rob and I walked by one of the kitchen tents, several college students asked if we could help build some tables for food preparation. Oh goodness, did they ask the right guys! We went and got our tools and our goggles and masks. We were working with several young college students who had come for the weekend from Lacrosse, Wisconsin, and were sleeping in tents. Haley, the young woman who helped me with my table told me that her parents didn't know she was there (it was hard for me to keep from trying to convince her to contact her parents!). But I told them that it is so important, and how much I admired them, that they went to where the action is, to where history is being made.

On Sunday, I felt sick, so I was in the trailer most of the day, praying that I didn't have to be sick in that tiny trailer bathroom. Sunday night, Rob came back to the trailer and said that the medical tent a couple hundred yards away looked like a MASH unit.

People were streaming in with hypothermia, the effects of tear gas, and bruises—even open wounds—from rubber bullets and bean bags. He showed me a picture of one of the bullets. So we took several space blankets to the tent and went back to the trailer and watched streaming video of protestors and fire hoses, and other chaos that made my tummy hurt even more.

The pipeline has various issues around it and I'm not going to go into all of them here. To strip away all context and make this simply about where a pipeline should go is to ignore the history of this patch of land and the history between the people. What I experienced this past week was also more than a conflict between two sides of an issue. It was part of a larger conflict between two views of what the world is and what it should be.

The Native people I met represented a gathering of hundreds of tribes. They had a deeply respectful attitude toward one another, for us, for the land and the creation around us. They have a vision of a peaceful world. They questioned whether a certain amount of convenience was worth putting their earth and water at risk. "How much more do you people need? And do you really know the full cost?" Our Psalm this morning has a similar vision.

Jerusalem—built as a city

that is bound firmly together.
To it the tribes go up,

the tribes of the Lord,
as was decreed for Israel,

to give thanks to the name of the Lord.
For there the thrones for judgement were set up,

the thrones of the house of David.

Pray for the peace of Jerusalem:

'May they prosper who love you.
Peace be within your walls,

and security within your towers.'
For the sake of my relatives and friends

I will say, 'Peace be within you.'
For the sake of the house of the Lord our God,

I will seek your good. (122:3–9)

This was not written at a time of peace, but was the vision, the promise that kept people working for peace, for unity, for the security that comes in faith.

It is a statement of hope. And as Christians, we live expecting that God's promises of unity, peace, justice, and joy are true. We use this vision of a new world to help us decide what to do in our lives today.

Do any of you ever watch one of those movies or TV shows that feature time travel? What do they have to be careful of when they go back in time? (If they do something in the past it might change the future—their present.) That's pretty sobering: *everything* could change.

Well, imagine this: we are living in a moment of time in which what we do right now can change *everything* about the future. We are where the action is, where history is being made, right now.

And I don't just mean at Standing Rock, though I certainly do mean it too.

There are places in your life where you have more influence and more ability to bring changes than anyone else. It's your presence in that moment at that place, in your relationships, in your skills and special knowledge that can help feed the hungry, find the lost, and seek out the forgotten. No one else can do what you can.

Or maybe other people *could,* but they aren't. If you don't believe what you do can make a difference, if you don't have hope, you may never even try. And you won't be able to travel back in time for another chance at that moment.

You don't have to be able to travel back in time to change the future; you just have to be traveling forward at the same speed you are right now. This vision of what the world is meant to be and the hope that it will be, is what moves us, encourages us, and consoles us right now.

St. Augustine of Hippo said, "Hope has two beautiful daughters. Their names are anger and courage; anger at the way things are, and courage to see that they do not remain the way they are."

The forces of violence, hatred, and greed should make you angry. It takes courage to keep going, especially after losses and even mistakes. But hope is not passive. While it's the expectation that God will complete God's vision for the world, it's also our readiness to put ourselves to God's good use. Hope is not surrender to the way things are; it is the surrender of ourselves to God's dream of justice, peace, mercy, and love. As we sing this Advent season:

Come thou long Expected Jesus, born to set thy people free;
from our fears and sins release us, let us find our rest in thee.
Israel's strength and consolation, hope of all the earth, thou art.
Dear desire of every nation, joy of every longing heart.[1]

Let this vision of the future stir you to action and faith right now, so that history is made better because of you.

---

[1]Charles Wesley, "Come Thou Long Expected Jesus," 1744, public domain.

# 17

# Dependence Day: A Sermon for the Fourth of July

**Darryl Schafer**

Rev. Darryl Schafer is a counselor in Springfield, Missouri who specializes in working with those who have experienced religious trauma—those who have been deeply hurt by the messages they received as part of their religious experiences. He preached this sermon on July 3, 2016 at the Billings Christian Church (Disciples of Christ) in Billings, Missouri, where he served as pastor before becoming a full-time counselor.

• • •

*Galatians 5:13-15*

Tomorrow marks the day when we as a nation will eat more than what we should and participate in a collective act of forgetfulness. With the faint whiff of barbecue hanging in the air and the sight of controlled explosions lighting up the night sky, we as a nation will neglect our memory. We will gather together with family and friends to blind ourselves to our history, to neglect the foundations upon which this nation was built, and to perpetuate the myth of our independence.

I say "myth" because we the people have never truly been independent. Not really. We have forgotten our roots. We have forgotten where we come from. We have forgotten just how dependent we actually are—how dependent we have always been. We have forgotten who exactly we have depended upon to get us where we are today. In this collective act of forgetfulness at best and avoidance at worst, we will neglect to remember the source that has made America what it is today.

Before we go much further, let me say this: when I talk about the failure of our memory, that we are forgetting to whom we are indebted, I am not talking about God. This isn't that kind of sermon, one that calls America to remember its dependence upon our "Heavenly Father." If anything, even a cursory glance at the history of our nation shows that we haven't exactly been dependent on the Almighty.

No. We the people stand not upon the promises of God but upon a mountain several centuries in the making. A mountain piled high with the broken bodies of those whose blood cries out to God. Listen! Do you hear what God hears? Do you hear the cries of those who bear witness to a long train of "abuses and usurpations?"[1] Do you hear how their voices rise against the myth of our independence? Do you hear the demand that we acknowledge the ways in which we have been violently dependent upon the lives and bodies of those that have been broken beneath the wheels of history? Lives and bodies that refuse to stay silent? Lives and bodies that cry out, forcing us to critically reflect upon the way in which we have been dependent upon them?

Dependent on the genocide of the Native Americans whose land we stole in order to meet our insatiable demand for natural resources and to perpetuate the myth that private property is the highest good.

Dependent on the commodification, torture, and massacre of black lives, a system that leaves strange fruit hanging in the trees even today.

Dependent on the subjugation of women like my great-grandmother, who lived during a time when it was illegal for her to vote and who was paid less than a man for doing the same work (a trend that continues even today).

Dependent on the migrant workers who risk their lives to do the work that many Americans are unwilling to do, and often (always) for a fraction of the pay.

Dependent on the marginalization and continued bigotry against those in the LGBTQ+ community.

Dependent on the xenophobia that allows us to inflict and justify untold cruelty toward Muslims inside and outside our borders.

Dependent on the belief that America can do no wrong and that the rest of the world should just quit whining when we kill their children with our weapons of mass destruction.

Dependent on the sense of entitlement and consumption that permits a few to have more than what they need at the expense of many having less than what they need.

We are, in no way, independent. We are very much dependent upon the immeasurable violence we are capable of levying against others. What makes America "great" again and again is our time-honored belief—clearly exhibited throughout our history—that not all lives matter.

And yet . . . I still hold out hope. I still believe in the messages that come our way now and then. Of those who dare to hold the mirror up to America's collective gaze. Of those who climb flagpoles to rip down the stars and bars that attempted to bar black people from standing in their

God-given dignity. Of those who say that Muslims are just as much the children of God as Christians. Of those who proclaim that God's children come in every color and every expression of the rainbow. Of those who dare to dream that what is does not necessarily stand as what must be.

If I may invoke the preacher, I, too, have a dream.

A dream where we no longer idolize those who founded this country. A dream where we no longer perpetuate the sins of our Founding Fathers, a group of wealthy, white men who were as equally guilty of the charge that they levied against their own king, namely that they, too, "obstructed the Administration of Justice."[2]

I have a dream today. A dream where we confess our dependence upon the violence to which we have turned a willfully ignorant eye, where we repent of the forgetful spirit of our age, and heed the call to hear what God hears—the blood of our brothers and sisters crying out from the ground upon which we stand.

A dream where independence is more than some sacralized myth but is instead a future that is hoping, sighing, and dreaming to be born among us in the present. A dream where independence is a call to become independent of the very things we have been dependent upon for so long. A call, in Christ, to repent of and atone for the racism, the elitism, the prejudice, the bigotry, the hatred, the greed, and the cruelty that have characterized the history of the Christian west for centuries. A call to live in gospel-centered responsibility to each and every person we encounter. A call to use our liberty not as a resource for self-indulgence but as an opportunity to serve one another through love.

This is our Independence Day—the day to come. The day we wait for. The day we work for. The day that is not yet here because it depends upon us answering the call that God issues to each of us.

May we have eyes to see and ears to hear. May we no longer walk in forgetfulness. May we remember, and in so doing, may we prove our faithfulness to the one who calls us to remember.

"You were called to liberty, dear ones. But you must never use your liberty as a resource for self-indulgence" (Gal. 5:13, author's translation).

---

[1]The quoted material is from the Declaration of Independence.
[2]Declaration of Independence.

# 18

# Jesus Christ for President

**Sandhya Jha**

Rev. Sandhya Jha is the director of the Oakland Peace Center in Oakland, California. Her books include *Transforming Communities: How People Like You Are Healing Their Neighborhoods* and *Pre-Post-Racial America: Spiritual Stories from the Front Lines.* This sermon was preached on November 26, 2017, at First Christian Church (Disciples of Christ) in Concord, California. [Editor's note: this is an edited version of a transcript of the original sermon. It began with Jha leading the congregation in singing the Woody Guthrie song, "Christ for President." Copyright laws don't allow us to republish the full lyrics here, but readers can view them online at the Woody Guthrie archive.[1]]

• • •

*Matthew 25:31–46*

*O It's Jesus Christ our President*
*God above our king*[2]

Thank you for being willing to do that song with me! It's a very little-known Woody Guthrie song, so it has a lot of history to it, and it's a song I love very much. It's fitting for today, since it's Christ the King Sunday (or Reign of Christ Sunday), which is New Year's Eve for the church.

The new church calendar starts next Sunday, with the first Sunday of Advent, as we prepare to welcome the baby Jesus into our lives and world. But today, on the last Sunday of the Christian year, we celebrate how Jesus is going to come again. In one tradition, it's called Doom Sunday! (Well, it used to be called Doom Sunday until they realized that was bad advertising, so they renamed it Return of Christ Sunday.)

Today's feast day goes back to 1925, and I want you to think about that time. It was in the shadow of World War I. Times were tough. Dictators

103

were beginning to rise to power. According to the United Methodist Church, Catholics in Mexico were being told they had to place all of their authority in the state. In turn, the pope created Christ the King Sunday to encourage the freedom of Catholics to practice their religion, to encourage world leaders to honor Jesus and not worship themselves, and also as a way for the church to stand in solidarity with people who were being harmed for following Jesus first and their country second. This commitment was more radical than even the pope realized.

If you think back to the Palm Sunday procession that Jesus was part of the week before he died, it was a piece of political theater. Jesus and his followers, and all of the regular folks in Jerusalem, were making fun of the emperor, whose procession was coming from the other side of the city, with all of its pomp and circumstance, and the centurions decked out in their fine garb. Jesus's little humble processional was making fun of the emperor for thinking he was a god. It was making fun of him for thinking that the military gear and the pageantry of war was where real power came from. It was making fun of the emperor for thinking his riches made him a king, when only God is king.

When Woody Guthrie wrote the song we sang this morning, he understood who Jesus really was. He wrote it during the McCarthy era, which used the fear of communism as a nefarious way of shutting down workers' rights, beginning to recreate the wealth inequity that we suffer under today, that was just beginning to be corrected after the Great Depression. So of course Woody Guthrie wrote that we needed to cast the money changers out of the temple and put the carpenter in. Woody Guthrie was a lot like the people in this church. He had a deep disdain for people who abused faith for the sake of power. He knew that "If Jesus was to preach [in New York City] like he preached in Galilee, [we] would lay [him] in his grave."[3]

Woody Guthrie grew up in Oklahoma, and he moved to California from Texas during the Dust Bowl of the Great Depression, leaving his wife and child behind in the hopes of earning enough money to send back to support them. He understood today's passage, calling on people to be sheep and not goats when others were suffering. But Woody Guthrie understood something that I didn't. I didn't understand it until our friend Dan Paul, the Disciples of Christ pastor in Pacific Grove, mentioned it to me. And it makes the reading of this story make so much sense on this Reign of Christ Sunday.

Are you ready for this? Maybe you all know this. I didn't know this. Jesus was calling on the people of Israel, as a nation, to be sheep and not goats. As an American who's been trained well into this mythology of the individual mattering more than the collective, I always read this story individually, as in "*I* need to be a sheep and not a goat." And our individual actions absolutely matter. But he was saying something much bigger than we have been trained to realize.

He was saying to his people, "Do you want to be like the government of Rome, which creates this suffering, which imprisons people for standing up for their rights, which leaves people unnecessarily hungry and creates conditions that make them sick? Or do you want to be *a* people, not just people, but *a* people, who cares for the sick, who visits those in prison, who feeds and clothes people in need? Which nation do you want to be? Which government do you want to be? Because I will not even recognize this nation that God ordained, if it cannot be a nation doing God's will."

Before asking you to do the song "Christ for President" with me today, I did a little research into our nation's most treasured folk singer, the man whose song "This Land Is Your Land" is one many of us have been singing since kindergarten. I knew Woody Guthrie had grown up in Oklahoma. I also knew that Oklahoma had the highest number of lynchings, per capita, of any state in this nation. I did not know that Guthrie's father, Charles Guthrie, participated in at least one lynching of a black mother and son. I did not know that Charles Guthrie joined the Klan when it was revitalized in the 1910s. Our goat nation had told Charles Guthrie that black people were his enemy, that they wanted what he had and he had to protect it from them, and he believed them. He believed his goat nation with a vengeance. Charles Guthrie sided with the goats, and he still lost everything in the Dust Bowl in Oklahoma. The thing Charles Guthrie didn't realize is that when things go badly for us, a goat government doesn't remember when we were on their side. Goats don't have our backs.

> He said to the rich, "Give your goods to the poor"
> So they laid Jesus Christ in His grave[4]

Jesus was not just giving us spiritual advice, although that would have been good advice. He was giving us sage counsel to have each other's backs because we never know when we'll need someone to have ours. A sheep nation is more faithful, but it is also the better long-term strategy for our own survival. Woody Guthrie struggled with living in a goat-led nation, but he knew his people were the sheep. Guthrie wrote songs about that lynching that his father participated in, condemning the act. He didn't pretend that history hadn't happened. His history, though, did not stop him from standing up fiercely against fascism and against racism and against harming workers, and standing up for a different version of Jesus than the politicians and preachers of the time were circulating.

That takes humility. And that's why this Sunday, whether you call it Reign of Christ Sunday or Christ the King Sunday, matters to me. You've heard me talk so many times about the spiritual discipline of humility, so how can I get up here and talk about Christ the King and his elevated status? Well, my favorite piece of sneaky language in "Christ for President" is "Cast your vote for the carpenter that they call the Nazarene." Not only were carpenters still not regarded with much respect when Guthrie wrote the song, but you know what it means when the people called Jesus a Nazarene? It was hurled as an insult: "Can anything good come from Nazareth?" they whispered. In the same way that Jesus rode humbly into Jerusalem on a donkey, turning on its head our notions of what power looked like, he got called the King from Nazareth, from where nothing good can come.

But what a nation we could be if we were a nation of humble sheep, and not punishing goats. The church had an opportunity in 1925, while the rise of fascism was within their sight and Nazism was on the horizon. What if Reign of Christ Sunday had meant an acknowledgment that Christ's sovereignty meant healing the sick, visiting those in prison, feeding the hungry, and clothing the naked?

At a moment now, when the nonviolent movement for black lives has been deemed a terrorist organization by our government (all while they turn a blind eye to the actual terrorism of white supremacy), let us take advantage of the opportunity that the church missed back in 1925. Let us proclaim the reign of Christ, a humble man, from the wrong side of the tracks, who came from people who had to work for a living, who healed and clothed and fed and visited. Let that be our benchmark, for true leadership, today and always. Amen.

---

[1]For lyrics, see "Christ for President," http://www.woodyguthrie.org/Lyrics/Christ_for_President.htm.

[2]"Christ for President."

[3]See especially his song, "Jesus Christ," http://woodyguthrie.org/Lyrics/Jesus_Christ.htm.

[4]"Jesus Christ."

# 19

# Nevertheless, She Persisted

**Richard Gehring**

Rev. Dr. Richard Gehring is copastor (with Rev. Barb Gehring) of Manhattan Mennonite Church in Manhattan, Kansas, where this sermon was preached on August 20, 2017. He earned his MDiv from Anabaptist Mennonite Biblical Seminary and DMin from McCormick Theological Seminary.

• • •

*Isaiah 56:1-8; Matthew 15:21-28*

"No matter where you're from, we're glad you're our neighbor." That's what it says on the sign out in front of our building. In fact, those words of welcome are written not only in English, but also in Spanish and Arabic. Like several others here, I have the same sign in my yard at home. And I'm always pleased to see others like it when I'm traveling around town.

These signs were created about a year ago in the midst of an electoral campaign where there was a lot of anti-immigrant rhetoric. Started by a church in Harrisonburg, Virginia, the sign can now be found in at least 40 different states, three Canadian provinces and the West African nation of Liberia. The message of welcome and inclusion is especially important to proclaim now in the aftermath of the violence perpetrated by white nationalists last weekend in Charlottesville—only about an hour's drive away from the church that first created the welcoming sign. The message is one that is firmly rooted in scripture. Our Old Testament text for this morning is a prime example of this message. The prophet Isaiah looks ahead to the day when every tribe and every nation will be a part of God's people. Those who were formerly barred from full participation in the community—eunuchs and foreigners—are welcomed.

It is a vision of an international body serving the Lord in obedience and offering praise to God in the harmony of many tongues: "For my house shall be called a house of prayer for all peoples" (Isa. 56:7). This sentence is one that Jesus himself quotes when he drives the money-changers out of the temple. It is, in fact, this action on behalf of welcoming everyone into God's house that ultimately gets him arrested, tried, and executed.

So I find it very puzzling and, frankly, quite disturbing to read about what he does in today's New Testament text where we find Jesus acting in what seems to be a very "un-Jesus-like" manner. In this passage, Jesus makes a rare excursion outside of Jewish territory into "the district of Tyre and Sidon," which would be present day Lebanon. And as soon as he arrives, he encounters a woman who desperately begs him to help her daughter who is possessed by a demon. So Jesus heals her. Actually, he doesn't do anything right away. At first, he completely ignores her. He doesn't respond at all until his disciples tell him to get rid of this pesky woman who keeps talking. And instead of rebuking them as he does when they try to keep parents from bringing their kids to him, he seems to agree with them by proclaiming that his ministry is "only to the lost sheep of the house of Israel." He doesn't seem to accept any responsibility toward this Canaanite woman by adopting a sort of "Israel first" policy. She, however, refuses to take "no" for an answer, continuing to plead, "Lord, help me" as she falls to her knees.

Initially, Jesus does not help this woman. Instead, he calls her—at least indirectly—a "dog." "It is not fair," he says, "to take the children's food and throw it to the dogs." To refer to someone as a "dog" was considered one of the worst names that could be applied to other people back in Jesus's day. But this woman simply will not go away. In the now infamous words of Senator Mitch McConnell, "She was warned. She was given an explanation. Nevertheless, she persisted." "Yes, Lord, yet even the dogs eat the crumbs that fall from their masters' table." At this point, Jesus relents. He gives in and says to her, "Woman, great is your faith! Let it be done for you as you wish." And Matthew reports that "her daughter was healed instantly."

It's a happy ending. But I'm left wondering, "Jesus, what took you so long? Why didn't you just heal her right away? Why did you ignore her? Why did you insult her?" It is a very troubling story. Jesus is reluctant to do what seems like the obvious thing to do—to respond to someone in great need with compassion and mercy. Instead, he waffles and waits and uses offensive language that seems so out of character.

To be certain, the woman has violated a whole range of social taboos by talking to Jesus. For one, women weren't supposed to talk to men. But Jesus violates that taboo by interacting with women on many other occasions. Another taboo said that Jews shouldn't mingle with Gentiles. Again, though, Jesus breaks this taboo repeatedly. He's already healed the servant of a Roman soldier—a commander of troops occupying his own nation. In taking such actions, we find echoes of stories from the Old Testament as well. We often tend to oversimplify our understanding of the Bible by declaring that the Old Testament is about "law" and the New Testament is about "grace." But the fact is that there is a strong movement toward grace in the Old Testament. There are numerous instances where God's grace and mercy are indeed extended beyond the borders of Israel. Elijah brought the son of the widow in Zarephath back to life. Elisha healed the Syrian commander Naaman of leprosy. And as I noted earlier, in today's Old Testament passage, Isaiah explicitly welcomes some of those who had formerly been seen as outside the law.

Jesus follows this long prophetic tradition of extending the boundaries to "outsiders" as he interacts with foreigners and lepers and women. In fact, earlier in this same chapter in Matthew, the Pharisees and scribes are critical of Jesus precisely because of his refusal to follow rules. He and his disciples violate the purity code by not washing their hands before they eat. Jesus's response to the Pharisees' complaint is found in the first part of our text for today, "[I]t is not what goes into the mouth that defiles a person, but it is what comes out of the mouth that defiles. . . . For out of the heart come evil intentions, murder, adultery, fornication, theft, false witness, slander. These are what defile a person, but to eat with unwashed hands does not defile" (Mt. 15:11, 19–20).

Given this pronouncement, it is all the more disconcerting to hear what does come out of Jesus's mouth just a few verses later when he refers to non-Israelites as "dogs." It sounds more like a tweet from Donald Trump than something Jesus would say. It's even more puzzling that Jesus defends his inaction by declaring that there isn't enough bread to share with this woman in need. This passage is literally sandwiched between two stories of amazingly abundant bread. So why is he now being so stingy with the bread of life that he has to offer?

I wish I had an answer to that question. I wish I could explain all the troubling aspects of this story. I wish I knew why he ignored her for so long. I wish I understood why he refused to help her at first. I really wish he hadn't used the term "dog." Frankly, I wish Jesus would have just done what he does in almost every other instance in the gospels: healed the woman as soon as she asked rather than dragging it out and being so resistant.

Ultimately, though, Jesus does heal the Canaanite woman's daughter. Ultimately, Jesus praises this woman's "great faith"—a term that he never uses for any other person. Ultimately, Jesus recognizes that his ministry does extend beyond just those who are already part of God's covenant. Ultimately, Jesus fulfills the prophecy of Isaiah, "I will gather others to them besides those already gathered" (Isa. 56:8). Ultimately, Jesus affirms that Canaanite lives matter. So maybe I don't need to understand exactly why he acted the way he did before he healed the woman's daughter. Maybe the question we should be asking is not, "Why was Jesus so reluctant to respond to the woman?" Maybe the more appropriate question is, "How can we follow his example in turning away from bigotry and privilege toward blessing and affirmation of those who are different?" If Jesus listened to women, shouldn't we?

We are understandably appalled by the scenes from Charlottesville, Virginia, last weekend. The images of young white men marching with torches, Confederate flags, and swastikas while wearing makeshift riot gear is indeed a chilling sight. For many, it is shocking that this could still happen in our country in the 21st century. Over the past week, many politicians, business leaders, activists, and members of the clergy have responded with condemnation to the violence perpetrated by white nationalists. Soon, however, the headlines about Charlottesville will recede. They'll be replaced by something else, just as those headlines replaced the threats from Kim Jong Un that were so omnipresent a mere 10 days ago. And just as many Americans have all but forgotten that we remain on the brink of a nuclear war with North Korea, so most will forget about the alt-right and the death of Heather Heyer—at least until the next incident of racial violence close to home.

But just as our nation's militarism continues to be a threat to world peace, so also is racism alive and well in this country. While it may have been more organized and larger than many other demonstrations, the uprising in Charlottesville was not the first incident of racial violence in recent months. Nor is it likely to be the last. Just within the past year, right here in Kansas, we've witnessed the murder of an Indian immigrant in Olathe, and the arrest of three men for plotting to blow up an apartment complex filled with Somalis in Garden City. Like many such stories across the nation, these incidents have raised questions of racism for a short time before fading again into the background. In fact, the way that a lot of these stories get told only serves to perpetuate certain ideas that keep us from actually dealing with the racism that lives on in much more subtle ways.

Let's face it: there are very few Americans who will proudly display a swastika or chant, "Jews will not replace us." There are very few Americans who will take up a gun or a bomb and actively seek out immigrants or people of other faiths to kill them. So it's fairly easy to take a stand against such blatantly racist acts. Of course, that's what makes it all the more troubling when the president fails to do so and is supported in his vague statements by very visible religious leaders like Franklin Graham and Jerry Falwell Jr. Tweeting our outrage at neo-Nazis and the alt-right is fairly simple. It is far more difficult to work at dismantling the much deeper levels of racism embedded within our society. A society that broke treaties and stole land from Native Americans. A society that was built on the backs of African slave labor. A society that told white Anglo-Saxon Protestants, "Give me your tired, your poor, your huddled masses yearning to be free," but has consistently resisted welcoming others from Irish Catholics to Russian Jews to Somali Muslims and from Chinese laborers to Mexican farm workers to Syrian refugees.

Working against that long history of racism is challenging. But there are plenty of opportunities. One of the ways that I plan to step up in that effort is by attending the Mass Meeting tomorrow night in Topeka. On our last sabbatical three years ago, Barb and I had the opportunity to hear Rev. William Barber, who will be speaking. When I saw him then, I recognized Rev. Barber as the closest embodiment of Dr. Martin Luther King Jr. of anyone I've ever encountered. Now, Rev. Barber has picked up on the very project that King himself was working on when he was murdered: The Poor People's Campaign. It is almost exactly 50 years since Dr. King delivered his often overlooked "Three Evils of Society" speech in which he denounced "the triple prong sickness . . . of racism, excessive materialism and militarism." It is these very evils that the new Poor People's Campaign is seeking to cure. I hope many of the rest of you will be there as Rev. Barber kicks off the effort right here in Kansas. But if you can't make it, rest assured that you will be hearing about it from me and from others in the congregation as we look to implement efforts to create a more just society and live more fully into the reign of God.

We who are "good white people" like to think that we don't harbor racism within us. But we often fail to recognize the ways in which we continue to perpetuate prejudice and discrimination. Let me put it this way: if even Jesus—the Son of God, the incarnate Word, the Savior of the World—if even he struggled with bigotry and privilege, then who are we to think that racism, or patriarchy, has no effect on us? Jesus also provides us then with a model for how to overcome and transform our prejudices and presuppositions. For Jesus allows himself to be taught by a woman on the fringes—this foreigner whom he's not supposed to even be listening to. Jesus humbles himself by submitting to the will of the Canaanite woman. One commentator describes what happens this way:

> Jesus the Human One, was human enough to have his Jewish male privilege with all its racism, pierced by plight of a poor and desperate woman who came from an enemy people. The glory is that Jesus, despite his privilege, was still able to be merciful; able to choose the way of God—and that he did. The glory is that when he understood what he had done, and how he had behaved, he changed instantly, and healed the daughter of the woman; he fed her, just as he had fed his Jewish sisters and brothers.[1]

This morning, we gather at the table of the Lord to also be fed by Jesus. We are invited to feast on the Bread of Life, not forced to lick the crumbs that fall on the floor. Though we may be unworthy—though we struggle to overcome the systemic racism and patriarchy that grip our society—Jesus invites us to the table, declaring to us, "No matter where you are from, I'm glad you're my neighbor."

---

[1]Andrew Prior, "Blind Privilege and the Kingdom of Heaven," https://www.onemansweb.org/blind-privilege-and-the-kingdom-of-heaven-matthew-1510-28.html.

# 20

# Did Mary Say "Me Too"?

**Wil Gafney**

Rev. Dr. Wil Gafney, an Episcopal priest, is an associate professor of Hebrew Bible at Brite Divinity School in Fort Worth, Texas. She's the author of *Womanist Midrash: A Reintroduction to Women of the Torah and of the Throne* and *Daughters of Miriam: Women Prophets in Ancient Israel* and coeditor of *The Peoples' Bible* and *The Peoples' Companion to the Bible.* This reflection was originally posted to her blog on November 26, 2017, and adapted for this collection.

• • •

*Luke 1:26–37*

Did the Blessed Virgin say, "Me too"? There is a moment in the Annunciation story when an ordinary girl on the cusp of womanhood is approached by a powerful male figure who tells her what is going to happen to her body, in its most intimate spaces. (#MeToo is a collection of women's stories acknowledging their experiences of sexual assault and harassment following very public claims against a number of media executives.)

Sit with me in this moment, this uncomfortable moment, before rushing to find proof of her consent, or argue that contemporary notions of consent do not apply to ancient texts, or God knew she'd say yes so it was prophetic, or contend that (human) gender does not apply to divine beings, Gabriel or God, or the Holy Spirit's feminine anyway. Hold those thoughts and just sit in the moment with this young woman.

Even in the Iron Age in an androcentric and patriarchal culture, she knows her body belongs to her. She doesn't ask what her intended will say, what her father will say, what about the shame this would likely bring on her, her family, and their name. Instead she testifies to the integrity of her body under her control. In her question, "How can this be?" I hear, "Since I have not done and will not do what you are suggesting—just in case you are really here to defraud me and my intended—how will this thing work?" I see her withholding consent at this moment. She has questions and has not agreed to this, glorious messianic prophecy notwithstanding. Not yet.

It's in this moment between "this is what you will do, what will happen to and in your body," and submission to what she accepts as God's will that I ask, Does Mary say, "Me too"? Does she have a choice here? The narrative and world that produced it may well say no. That is what makes this a "me too" story to me.

Yet in a world that did not necessarily recognize her sole ownership of her body and did not understand our notions of consent and rape, this very young woman had the dignity, courage, and temerity to question a messenger of the Living God about what would happen to her body before giving her consent. That is important. That gets lost when we rush to her capitulation. Before Mary said, "yes," she said, "wait a minute, explain this to me."

After the holy messenger explains the mechanics of the conception that is to take place—he is still saying, "this will happen to you"—then and only then does she consent, using the problematic language of the text and her world, "Indeed, I am the woman-servant-slave of the Lord (a slaveholding title)." Mary's submission is in the vernacular of slavery, as is much of the gospel. The language of "servitude" is a misnomer in biblical translation; even though they were not necessarily enslaved in perpetuity, they were enslaved. And while enslaved had no right to protect the integrity of their bodies or control of their sexuality or reproduction. We often soften the language to "servant" particularly with reference to God but the language of slavery runs through the whole Bible and is often found without critique on the lips of Jesus.

In this light, her consent is troubled and troubling: "let it be with me according to your word." Given what we know about power dynamics and hierarchy (not to mention the needs of the narrative), how could she have said anything else? I think that there is not much difference between "overshadowed" and "overwhelmed." I also remember Jeremiah saying God had seduced[1] and overpowered[2] him.

Did the Ever-Blessed Virgin Mary say, "Me too?" Perhaps not. A close reading shows her presumably powerless in every way but sufficiently empowered to talk back to the emissary of God, determine for herself, and grant what consent she could no matter the power of the One asking. And yet in that moment after being told by someone else what would happen to her body, she became not just the Mother of God, but the holy sister to those of us who do say, "Me too."

---

[1] Translated as "enticed" in Jeremiah 20:7, פתה means "seduced" in Exodus 22:16, Deuteronomy 11:16, and Judges 14:15.

[2] The second verb, קזח, is one of two primary terms for rape in the Hebrew Bible.

# 21

# Deacon, Apostle, and Mother of God

**Micki Pulleyking**

Rev. Dr. Micki Pulleyking is ordained in the Christian Church (Disciples of Christ), teaches religious studies at Missouri State University, and serves as the minister of Westminster Presbyterian Church in Springfield, Missouri. She preached this sermon on February 12, 2016, for the Lenten series at Immaculate Conception Catholic Church, also in Springfield.

• • •

*Mark 14:3–9; Romans 16:1–7*

A *woman* enters Simon's house during dinner and pours oil on Jesus's head; it's an act of worship. This woman recognized Jesus as the Messiah and her action begins the passion of Christ, by preparing his body.

This sermon is written in memory of *her,* whose name is lost. The name of Jesus's betrayer is remembered; *her* name, this faithful disciple, is forgotten. May we remember the many forgotten women in the margins of our scriptures—women whose names we do not know but whose actions are significant, including the Syrophoenician woman, the widow who gave it all, the Samaritan woman . . . and the *48 additional women who are unnamed,* yet their place in sacred scripture, their lives, matter.

There are *35 different women who are named* in the New Testament. Besides the two Marys, how often are the other 33 women remembered in sermons? In this sermon, we shall remember a few New Testament women.

*Her name is Mary.* Imagine a young girl, a teenager, with long dark hair. Imagine her surprise. Luke includes women more often than any other gospel. In Luke 1, the angel comes to Mary (in Matthew, to Joseph). The angel says to Mary, "Greetings, favoured one! The Lord is with you" (Lk. 1:28).

She is addressed in exalted terms, implying, like great men in the Hebrew Bible, she has been chosen by God, empowered by God, and as some ancient texts add, "blessed among women" to give birth to God incarnate . . . to become the Mother of God!

*Her name is Elizabeth*, an older, pregnant woman who was unable to have children earlier in life. When Elizabeth gives birth to John the Baptist she names her son John. Naming rights means you have a position of power, thus the neighbors do not believe the words of a mere woman. Luke 1:43 says they are "astonished" when her husband, Zechariah, agrees with her.

Mary Magdalene, Joanna, and Susanna are named in Luke 8:1–3 for their role in financially supporting Jesus's ministry. Jesus has to eat. There is no indication he is employed. Joanna is wealthy and married to an influential man who manages the household of Herod Antipas. Joanna has connections.

Mary most likely comes from Magdala, a town with textiles, dyes, and a thriving fishing industry. Mary most likely is older, perhaps a widow, free to travel without a husband or children to care for. This is a very different image from the one European male artists create, whereby Mary is painted as a young, fair skinned, red haired prostitute with large breasts. (The scripture says nothing about Mary Magdalene being a prostitute. And red hair? No.) Mary will have a prominent role throughout Jesus's ministry, and in the early church, as we will see later.

The nameless woman at the well. Imagine Jesus talking to a woman about religion. Radical? Rabbi Eliezer said, "If a man teaches his daughter Torah it's as if he taught her lechery."[1]

Jesus taught women, though tradition in antiquity said "it was better to burn a scroll of the Torah than to allow a woman to study it."[2] Jesus talked with this nameless woman about . . . theology.

We do not know her name, but we do know this is the longest conversation in all of the Gospels—and it's between Jesus and a woman! Jesus initiates the conversation by asking her for a drink (Jn. 4:7). The Samaritan woman is greatly surprised that Jesus is speaking to her (Jn. 4:8). Jesus wants to chat with her about God; and their conversation is filled with spiritual metaphors. Then it happens. Jesus declares, for the first time, he is the Messiah (Jn. 4:26). John writes, "Just then his disciples came. They were astonished that he was speaking with a woman, but no one said, 'What do you want?' or, 'Why are you speaking with her?'" (Jn. 4:27). The woman understood Jesus's use of metaphor but the disciples did not. "Give me this living water!" she responds (cf. Jn. 4:15). This unnamed woman was the first Gentile missionary to Samaria. John writes in 4:39, "Many Samaritans from that city believed in him because of the woman's testimony."

*Her name is Martha.* How many sermons have you heard on the great confession of . . . Martha! "I believe you are the Messiah, the Son of God, the one coming into the world," Martha says (Jn. 11:27). And according to John, *she* is the first. Martha's confession has been overlooked, while the Catholic Church was founded on a similar confession of Peter. Can we imagine St. Martha's basilica?

Nameless Roman woman, defined by her husband, Pilate, a government official. She has a dream about Jesus and in spite of opposition, she writes (thus, she is literate) a note of protest during Jesus's trial (Mt. 27:19), asking her husband Pilate not to have anything to do with the innocent man. But Pilate refuses to listen to her. Women must continue to write words of protest.

Nameless women at the cross. As we come to the end of Jesus's ministry, this remembrance is sad. While the male disciples denied Jesus, the women (though mostly unnamed) remain loyal through the dark agonies of the cross. Matthew, Mark, nor Luke mentions a single man at the cross, but all four Gospels conclude the narrative of the crucifixion by referring to the women who remained with Jesus until the end.

In all four Gospels, women discover the empty tomb! But, when the women tell of their discovery, the Gospel writers add the phrase, "The men did not believe the women." Jesus first reveals himself as the Messiah to the Samaritan woman; and it's to a woman that Jesus is first revealed as the risen Christ.

In John 20, it's to Mary Magdalene. Mary discovers the empty tomb; she then runs and tells Peter and another disciple; they look in the tomb and see that, yes, indeed, the body is gone! Then, the guys, go home! Mary stays. By the tomb. Weeping. Jesus asks her why, and she does not recognize him, until he says her *name*, "Mary!" (Names matter.) From that moment on, the course of human history is changed. "Rabbi!" Mary shouts. Jesus gives her a great commission to go and tell the gospel story. He entrusts her with the gospel message. She goes and declares (preaches) to the others, "I have seen the Lord" (Jn. 20:18). Does this story, along with the woman at the well, give a clue as to what Jesus would think about women preaching?

What about women apostles? The writings attributed to Paul indicate in order to be an apostle one must have seen the risen Lord and received a commission (1 Cor. 9:1–2; Gal. 1:11–17). Luke adds that one must have accompanied Jesus during his ministry (which the apostle Paul did not do). Mary meets the job requirements for an apostle. What? Had Mary's apostleship been accepted by the church, might the history of misogyny in Christendom be different?

Of all the women—both named and unnamed—in scripture, the two Marys are the best known, and the least known. Consider what they are "known" for: the Virgin Mary is known, and praised, for her nonsexual body. Yet Matthew 13:55–56 indicates Mary was not always a virgin; though unnamed, Jesus's sisters are mentioned: "Is not this the carpenter's son? Is not his mother called Mary? And are not his brothers James and Joseph and Simon and Judas? And are not all his sisters with us?"

Mary Magdalene is known for her oversexual body; but the prostitute theory is a made-up myth! There is no hope for progress until we see the sin of defining women by their sexuality.

How about all those women who were leaders in the church in Rome?

*Her name is Phoebe*, a deacon. As we read in Romans 16:1–2: "I commend to you our sister Phoebe, a deacon of the church at Cenchreae, so that you may welcome her in the Lord as is fitting for the saints, and help her in whatever she may require from you, for she has been a benefactor of many and of myself as well."

It's *deacon* in the Greek. Not deaconess. In the early 1600s, King James's committee decided to call Phoebe a "servant" because the idea of a woman being a deacon threatened the ecclesiology and structure of the Church of England. (Subsequent translators have restored Phoebe to her office.) Church tradition almost destroyed any memory of the last woman we will remember.

*Her name is Junia*; she is an apostle. Romans 16:7 reads, "Greet Andronicus and Junia, my relatives who were in prison with me; they are prominent among the apostles, and they were in Christ before I was." Junia was recognized as a woman apostle for the first 1500 years of Christian history. In the fourth century the famous church father, John Chrysostom, wrote about Junia: "[T]o be an apostle is something great. But to be outstanding among the apostles—just think of what a wonderful song of praise that is! They were outstanding on the basis of their works and virtuous actions. Indeed, how great the wisdom of this woman must have been that she was even deemed worthy of the title apostle."[3]

After the Reformation commentators began to add an "s" to the name Junia, to create a masculine name; they did not think it possible for a woman to be an apostle, as previous writers had assumed. Fortunately in the 20th century Junia was reclaimed by translators and we are able to celebrate her today.

There are many more women in Christian scripture, both named and unnamed. We honor the words of Jesus by remembering *her* story. We give hope to all humans and to the church by claiming *her* place at the table of Simon in the first century and at the table of Christ in the 21st.

May the church remember the first Gentile missionary, the first commissioned to tell the good news of the risen Christ and may we continue to tell and live the good news of dignity and equality for all persons.

In parables, Jesus chooses women to represent the action of God: "The kingdom of heaven is like yeast that a woman took and mixed in with three measures of flour until all of it was leavened" (Mt. 13:33). The parable of the lost coin tells of the woman who searches all day until she finds her lost coin (Lk. 15:8).

May we humans, together, represent the actions of God in the world. May we work together, serving each other, to create a just and equal earth.

May we celebrate the faith of our mothers and the faith of our fathers who have passed on the gospel to us, and may it be told, as Jesus said, "in memory of her."

---

[1]See Joachim Jeremias, *Jerusalem in the Time of Jesus* (Minneapolis: Augsburg Fortress, 1969), 373.

[2]Jeremias, *Jerusalem in the Time of Jesus,* 373n70.

[3]See Bernadette Brooten, "Junia . . . Outstanding among the Apostles," in Leonard Swidler and Arlene Swidler, *Women Priests: A Catholic Commentary on the Vatican Declaration* (Mahwah, NJ: Paulist Press, 1977), 141.

# 22

# Rachel Weeps for Her Children: A Sermon of Restoration

**Alexis James Waggoner**

Rev. Alexis James Waggoner is an ordained minister in the Christian Church (Disciples of Christ). She's the Marketing and Digital Education Director for the Westar Institute, founder of the Acropolis Project, and chaplain in the Air Force Reserves. The sermon was preached at Dover Air Force Base Chapel on December 18, 2016.

• • •

*Matthew 2:16–18*

I think the year that Advent came "easiest" to me was a few years ago when I was pregnant with my daughter; I was definitely waiting in expectation! Being pregnant was the most expectant I'd ever been, especially as my due date drew near.

If you're like me, it's a lot easier to get wrapped up in these here-and-now expectations and longings than it is to feel anticipatory about the season of Advent. I've tried to *make* myself feel anticipatory and I've done it to both extremes. I used to think that more, more, more meant I was "winning" at celebrating Christmas. But over the last couple of years I've tried to scale it back to just a few purposeful things that I hope help us as a family calm down and prepare for the season of waiting.

Along the way I've had to ask myself, "What are we preparing for?" I think it's hard to be anticipatory because we think we know what's coming. Most of us—Christian or not—"know" the story of the angels, and Mary, and Joseph, and Jesus, and the stable, the shepherds, the wise men. We aren't excited, or hopeful, or fearful about how that's all going to play out.

But there's something that often gets overlooked in the Christmas story. In the middle of Matthew's telling of Christ's arrival (Mt. 2), there is this tragic, upsetting passage featuring Herod's slaughter of the innocents, accompanied by Rachel's weeping for her lost children. Herod—in an attempt after Jesus's birth to eradicate any threats of another "king"—has boys two years old and under slaughtered. Right there in the middle of the Christmas story about hope, peace, and joy. And Rachel—one of the ancient Israelite matriarchs—is weeping and *refusing to be consoled.*

Rachel's appearance in the story is a nod to the Hebrew Bible and the Book of Jeremiah (Jer. 31). Jeremiah spans a relatively long period of time in Israel's history. After the rule of Solomon, Israel splits into two kingdoms because of a dispute about who should be the next king. Over the generations there are some good rulers in these two kingdoms, but most of the kings are deemed "evil" by those prophesying. Jeremiah is a text comprised of many of these prophesies. Eventually, the prophets tell us—as a result of doing wickedly in God's eyes—the Northern and Southern Kingdoms are both invaded and conquered. But "conquered" doesn't mean "destroyed" entirely. A remnant stays in Israel, and a decent number of Israelites are taken captive and exiled into the conquering nations.

This is the reality into which Jeremiah speaks. Rachel, the wife of Jacob, is used as the embodiment of the nation's anguish over beloved Israelites lost to the fighting, the conquering, the exile. She gives voice to pain and suffering endured by the nation. But Jeremiah doesn't let it lie there. As we read in chapter 31,

> Thus says the LORD:
> Keep your voice from weeping,
>     and your eyes from tears;
> for there is a reward for your work,
> says the LORD:
>     they shall come back from the land of the enemy.
> (31:16)

Rachel, refusing to be consoled, is met with hope and promise from God.

We tend to read into this a figurative Christian interpretation that points to Christ. But we're not there yet. We need to first take the text on its own terms. Rachel is weeping and God is promising a literal, physical return and renewal of her family through (as the rest of the passage—and the book of Jeremiah—explains) a return from exile. And the exiles do return. They eventually come back to worship, to rebuild their temple, to receive the promise God is making here to Rachel.

And then she shows up again in Jesus's story in Matthew. She definitely has the only understandable response to the destruction Herod has visited on so many Egyptian families. She is weeping and refusing to be consoled. What could console you after the loss of your child? This scenario is quite literally my worst nightmare. Rachel's presence in the story tells us something important: there is room for extreme sadness and inconsolable loss in the midst of the Advent story—a story that is normally shared with hope and joy.

I think this loss and hope are *required* to go hand-in-hand. If the Advent of Hope, Peace, Joy, and Love doesn't meet those who are in their deepest sorrow, it isn't a Word worth waiting for. And perhaps this is why it's hard for me to feel truly expectant as we wait on Christ: perhaps I don't truly believe that Christ, the Word made flesh, will show up for me, my loved ones, my community, in the moments of our pain. The Word that we wait for has to have something to say to Rachel, weeping for her children—to us, when we are broken by injustice, when we are demoralized by the headlines, when we are exhausted in our resistance. The hope we wait for has to say, along with Jeremiah, that these losses will be restored.

In Jeremiah, Rachel gets to experience a physical renewal: the literal presence of her children returning home. In using Rachel as an emblem for suffering, and in using Jeremiah as the prophetic text, I think the author of Matthew is implying that we, in Christ's presence and promise, can expect the same. Yes, we can expect and anticipate God's future kingdom on earth with no more suffering, pain, and sorrow.

But we can also expect glimpses of that kingdom now. Not just in an eschatological future that we anticipate, but in the way we inhabit the world today; in the "already-but-not-yet."

Perhaps this is the anticipatory message of Advent.

Christ has already come, we know this story—the manger, Bethlehem, no room at the inn. And we know that the work of renewal has begun. But Christ is not yet here—and we are called to join God in Christ's renewal work until such a time as it is no longer necessary. I don't know what the sorrows are in your life, I don't know where you're joining Rachel with inconsolable weeping. I do know there is expectation that sorrow is not the last word. And that expectation is not just for the future Kingdom, it's for our messy, beautiful, human lives in the here and now.

# 23

# There Is Nothing New under the Sun

---

**Jesse Jackson**

Rev. Jesse Jackson is the pastor of East Sixth Christian Church (Disciples of Christ) in Oklahoma City, Oklahoma, where this sermon was preached on October 22, 2017. As a community organizer, teacher, and minister, he's been the recipient of numerous awards including, most recently, the Oklahoma Conference of Churches 2017 Advocacy Award. He has served on the executive committee of Black Lives Matter Oklahoma, was the principle organizer and convener of Occupy the Corners OKC, and former president of the National Convocation of the Christian Church (Disciples of Christ).

• • •

*Ecclesiastes 3:15-16*

It's remarkable how familiar much of what we are experiencing now seems. We are faced with a racist and an oppressive regime in the White House. Indifferent and oppressive language not only comes out of the mouth of our president, but it's embraced and encouraged by many in our society.

There is a blatant disrespect for life, particularly black life, and dealing with one another as equals seems like a lost art. Folks want to dominate rather than dialog. And when you try and engage in dialog, they call you divisive. It seems like I've read about this time before, in my history books. Have we gotten in a political and social time machine?

I've asked myself, "How did our elders and our ancestors make it in a mean world? How did they survive when it appeared that the entire world was against them? How did they maintain faith in God and humanity when their sisters and brothers were being lynched, excluded, and openly discriminated against? How did they manage to pray, preach, sing, and praise? What made them fight for a country that kept them as second class citizens?"

I can only deduce that God made some of the most remarkable people to ever walk the face of the earth. We are the evidence that our ancestors survived. Even in the teeth of the most brutal form of chattel slavery this planet has ever seen, they survived. Denied the right to learn to read and write, they survived. They separated husband from wife and children from parents, but they survived. The only part of the Bible the oppressors wanted us to know was "Slaves, obey your earthly masters" (Col. 3:22), but somehow, we survived.

We are the recipients of an incredible spirit; we've been given remarkable genes from our foreparents and from God. Our ancestors might not have expected to see freedom for themselves in the land of the living, yet they prayed that we would. They never met us, yet they prayed for us. They prayed that God would grant us, who they would never meet, what had been denied them in their life. There were those who would never taste freedom, but they believed that one day, their descendants would.

That's a faith that the devil don't know what to do with and one that we need to reclaim. Our text from Ecclesiastes says, "That which is, already has been . . ." In other words, we've seen this before; "there is nothing new under the sun" (Eccl. 1:9).

During the election cycle, we could see the handwriting on the wall. We knew what type of racial climate awaited inauguration day. Nazis and Klansmen came out of their holes and felt that they had their man in the White House. They no longer had to hide who they were. They were able to do and to say whatever they wanted without rebuke from those in charge.

So on election night, I, like so many of you, wondered aloud, "What are we going to do now?" (It might not have been so bad had we not come off eight years of the grace and dignity of President Obama.) We went from grace to disgrace; from class to crass; from dignified to a dunce. It was a tough pill to swallow. I prayed to God, "What are we going to do now?" And shortly after I asked that question, God answered, "We have seen this before." And God took my hand and walked me back in time to one of my favorite periods, the Harlem Renaissance.

Around the end of World War I (with a president viewing *Birth of a Nation* in the White House); two decades after Plessy v. Ferguson (which said that black people had no rights that white people were bound to respect); through horrible massacres like Black Wall Street in Tulsa, black people unleashed on the world what in my mind is the greatest creative period in the history of this nation.

During all of this turmoil, the artists inspired. Writers wrote with passion; singers sang with passion; musicians played with passion. Langston Hughes, Paul Robeson, Zora Neal Hurston, Wallace Thurman, Countee Cullen, Duke Ellington, Ethel Waters, Bessie Smith, Josephine Baker, Charlie Christian, Charley Patton, Robert Johnson, Thomas Dorsey, Leroy Alain Locke, and so many others got busy defining a generation. They gave the world the Charleston dance and the Lindy Hop. They gave the world swing music and bebop. They gave the world words that we are still reciting today. It was a creative genius that gave people hope in hopeless situations.

And while the artists were inspiring, Marcus Garvey was creating the largest organization of black people this nation has ever seen. W. E. B. Du Bois was helping give birth to the NAACP, which in turn gave us the Legal Fund, which gave us Thurgood Marshall. A. Philip Randolph was organizing sleeping car porters; Ida B. Wells was crusading against lynching. Roscoe Dunjee was telling the world how it is here in Oklahoma and Adam Clayton Powell was inspiring the movement with his words.

We've been here before.

The next part of our Bible verse says, "that which is to be, already is." This requires faith, because we don't always know how we are going to come out of our situation. But like our ancestors, we've got to have faith that God is going to work it out. God has given us everything we need to be successful; everything we need to make it through. God lets us know there is no need for us to look for answers outside our own history. Everything that God has done before, God will do again. God brought us out of Jim Crow because we prayed and worked. God brought us out of slavery because we prayed and fought for our own freedom. God won't do for us what we aren't willing to do for ourselves—but somewhere I read that *we can do all things through Christ who strengthens us* (Phil. 4:13); somewhere I read that *no weapon formed against us shall prosper* (Isa. 54:17).

The next verse from our text from Ecclesiastes says, "I saw under the sun that in the place of justice, wickedness was there, and in the place of righteousness, wickedness was there as well" (3:16). *There is nothing new under the sun.* Everything that we witness now, we have seen before. It's our expectations that got us. We expected that at this point in our history, we would no longer have to fight. We expected that in the 21st century, it ought to be self-evident to everybody how to treat one another. We expected that after 20 centuries we would know the importance of loving one another and the destructive power of hate.

But we know that the same God that was with our ancestors through their struggle is with us now. In the same way they struggled and fought for future generations, we must struggle and fight for those now and for those to come. We don't make it to the point that we no longer have to fight—in this world. We don't get a chance to let others do it for us—in this world. All of us have a role to play. Before us came artists and organizers and orators and supporters, and we carry this mantle. God is raising us up for such a time as this. There is nothing new under the sun. If we can no longer use our feet, we can use our wisdom. As Dr. King famously said, "If you can't fly then run, if you can't run then walk, if you can't walk then crawl, but whatever you do you have to keep moving forward."

We are the recipients of an incredible spirit. With the past behind us and the future in front of us, we will, like our ancestors, forge a way out of no way. We will struggle and fight for our future. God inspired our ancestors, and God will inspire us. We will make it through.

# 24

# Schadenfreude

**Anna M.J. Holloway**

Rev. Anna M. J. Holloway holds a MDiv from Phillips Theological Seminary and a master's of professional writing from the University of Oklahoma. She is approved for ordination in the United Church of Christ and is ordained in an independent church. She currently serves as director of the InterReligious Understanding program at Phillips, is a free-lance editor and writing teacher, and works in professional theatre in Oklahoma City. This sermon was preached at Cathedral of Hope United Church of Christ in Oklahoma City on September 24, 2017.

• • •

*Jonah 3:10–4:11; Matthew 20:1–16*

I need to teach you a word. Some of you already know it; if you have seen *Avenue Q* you know this word. It's "schadenfreude"—say it with me: "shah-den-froy-deh." It's a German word: "Freude" means joy, and in this particular context it means to find joy in the suffering of others. It's a very human characteristic, and we find ourselves doing this all the time. You're driving down the highway, and somebody cuts you off; it's frustrating, it's irritating, it's scary—you just barely avoided an accident! And you're very irritated about it!

And a mile later, you see the same guy got pulled over by the police, and they're getting a ticket! This big grin right here is what schadenfreude looks like—it doesn't matter that they deserved it; I'm still really thrilled that they got pulled over by the police.

And we do this all the time. We are perfectly normal creatures, God made us this way, we do this all the time.

In fact, our entire justice system has elements of schadenfreude all through it. We live with this lovely, simple idea that "justice" is about "punishment."

This guy breaks into your house and he steals your TV and your computer, and he runs off to sell them, and he gets caught. Well, I'm not

**125**

gonna get my door fixed, I'm not gonna get my window fixed, I'm not getting my computer or my TV back—but he gets to go to jail!! That's . . . justice.

Well, okay. That's how we work. It's also schadenfreude; we encourage the idea, in some ways in our culture, that we should expect this outcome, that we should feel good about it. This is justice! This man goes to jail, and that's yay! Superman in the cape. And that's what we're fighting for. Truth, justice, and the American way.

Here's the problem with that: we don't usually notice that the person damaged doesn't get much help fixing the damage, and the person in jail doesn't get much help reconnecting and becoming a more healthy person in the world. This version of "justice" doesn't make things better, really.

And still, this idea that some kind of punishment—retribution—is equal to "justice" is very human and very normal and all societies do some version of this.

But God—God doesn't do that. God doesn't do schadenfreude. God doesn't do "punishment equals justice" either, although there are many places where you will hear it preached. "If you behave badly," they thunder from the pulpit, "if you sin, you will be damned to eternal punishment, and this is what God WANTS for you!" Really? The merciful, all loving, all forgiving—all those accusations Jonah was making? You, see Jonah expects God to punish Nineveh. "You go all merciful," Jonah sneers. And yes, God does that. God does that! It's just so annoying! God gets so merciful with people! How do we put up with that? O.M.G.!!

Well, it's because we speak from an odd little place of privilege. There are all different kinds of privilege, and we all have different kinds of privilege, and not everybody has all privileges, and it's a tricky subject to talk about sometimes. But from some of our places of privilege, we tend to have expectations of "divine justice" that do not bear much resemblance to the way God acts.

Jonah is definitely a man of privilege. You understand that in the earlier parts of the story—the episodes we didn't get to hear—he has been asked by God to do this task, and he doesn't want to, so he decides to go on a cruise to Tarshish and he *pays the fare*—it says that in scripture: he pays the fare. That means he has money. Money is rare in the ancient world; people tended to pay with chickens and eggs and sheepskins and things like that or in other ways, with whatever they make. Trading in actual money was done with very small amounts most of the time. For him to have the cash to pack himself up with his suitcases and go to Tarshish at a moment's notice and pay for it, he's got *money*.

Jonah does not really want to go to Nineveh and stand there and deliver the word of God. He does not feel that this is the best use of his time. This is a businessman; I can understand how he feels. If he were to walk into Nineveh, in his three-piece suit and Armani tie, and stand there saying, "The Lord God is wroth with thee and will visit upon thee a calamity!"—I can imagine the people of Nineveh walking by and saying, "Who is this goober from out of town and where did he get the cool tie?"

So why he would do this? It's not going to help his business any; it's not going to make him more successful. So he says, "No, thanks, God—I'll take a cruise . . ." Only he doesn't get very far, and you know what happens: he gets barfed up on the shore, his clothes are in rags, he's lost all his luggage and he's soaking wet and smelling like fish guts. And he goes into town and he says, "God's mad at you and he's gonna dump stuff on you!" And the people of Nineveh look at him and say, "It looks like God has already started."

Okay, so possibly Jonah has a point—a little tiny one—thinking he wouldn't have been as effective if he'd gone right away when God asked. Maybe. We will never know—he didn't make that choice.

But he did eventually get to Nineveh, and according to scholars, probably didn't do much more than walk through town and grumble, "God's mad and there's trouble coming" and that's all.

And they listened to him. And they made a choice to repent. And they took it seriously.

Because God is not someone who is easy to fool. I mean, you can't just say, "We'll pretend to repent and God will leave us alone." It doesn't work that way.

So the people of Nineveh took it seriously, from the king all the way down the social ladder.

**But God did not smite them—they were not smote.**

And Jonah is peeved. He has had a whole string of bad days, and he wants his morning cup of hot steaming schadenfreude latte, and he's not getting it. So he's gonna go over here and sit in the desert and pout. Because he's mad. Because God was nice to people and he thought God should be mean to them.

This is what we do. We have expectations of how the universe should work, and it doesn't do what we want, and we pout. We say, "This is not fair!" This is what we do sometimes with our privilege.

We forget that "fair" for us isn't the same thing as "fair" for God.

So, thinking about that idea, we also look at the Matthew reading: the workers show up and negotiate for a day's pay, and they get a fair wage. Other workers show up; more workers show up later; along toward the end of the day, the last stragglers drag in. Then, they all get paid a full day's wage! And the people who are complaining are the ones who got what they asked for. Because—that's not fair. "It's not fair!" we say. "If I'd known I could have come in and been slovenly and worked only half a day for a full day's pay, I'd have done it!"

Now wait a minute. Even as the words come out of my mouth, I'm sitting here thinking, "Is that how I want to be thought of? 'Gee, if I could get by cheating people, I would do it'?" Really?

Whether they mean it that way or not, that's where they are coming from. There really are people complaining because they got what they negotiated for. And they don't think it was fair.

But the kingdom of God is like a vineyard where the master says, "I treat everybody the same. If I choose to be gracious to people, as long as you're not suffering for it, why are you upset? What's the problem?"

Well, it's like Jonah; he's sitting over here wanting his schadenfreude. "I came all the way from my nice home, and all the way through the stupid fish, and I ran all the way through Nineveh, and I didn't get to watch anybody suffer! Where are car chases? Where are the crashes and explosions? What kind of action movie is this?!!"

God doesn't work that way.

Jonah is wrong in a whole other way, and we miss this one too. Think of this as theater. In the story of Jonah, which is a teeny tiny little book in the Bible—and we know, by the way, that this is a story and not a piece of history because it doesn't start "Jonah, son of Joe, son of Fred, son of Sam . . ." It starts, "There was a man named Jonah," which is the old ancient Hebrew form of "Once upon a time . . ."

The whole book—the whole story—is Jonah. There's the backdrop with the city of Nineveh painted on it, and there's a little tiny scene where they say, "This is what they did in Nineveh." But all the front part—all the action of the play—is Jonah. So we forget what's going on in Nineveh; they're repenting in the painted backdrop while Jonah is out front pouting and demanding that God be mean to them.

So. What happens when you actually repent?

There are three stages of repentance, and the first one is, "Oh my gosh, I spilled my coffee." I'm aware I made a mistake. "I must clean it up." The second stage is repairing it. The third stage is the one we usually don't get to: "I should learn not to carry coffee in here." I should change my behavior so I don't make the mistake again. "I should carry a cup with a lid." I need to make a change to not do it again.

That's the hardest part, really, because you kind of figure the first part "Oh my gosh I'm aware of it" and "I'm sorry and I'm fixing it up"—that's enough, right? That will take care of it. That's plenty.

Things expand in our world. If you are dealing with a serious, serious issue, the kind that goes through a 12-step process, for example—all kinds of addictions and behavioral issues go through this kind of process—it's still three stages, but it's expanded into more steps because it's a much bigger issue to deal with.

You start when you come to an awareness: "Yes, I am behaving badly, and I have been behaving badly for a long time, and I've hurt a lot of people." The self-awareness comes first. And then you go into the second part of awareness, which is acknowledging to your friends and family that, "Yes, I am now aware that I've been a complete jerk and stupid and I've been doing all this bad stuff for years." And that has hitches because some of your family are going to say, "Oh, no, Honey, you're fine. Let me get you a drink." Because we know we have friends and relatives who are enablers. And then the other part of your extended family, when you go to them and say, "I'm now aware I've been doing all this" are the ones who are going to look at you and say, "Yeah, really? Like we didn't know? 'Cause we've been dealing with this for years. While you were pretending it wasn't happening. Great. Glad you finally know."

Okay. That's hard. That's harsh. And yet, by and large, the awareness part is actually the easiest part. Because the next part is the repair part. And there are all kinds of ways that an apology leads you toward repair, but you aren't really doing a repair unless you make an effort to actually, you know, repair.

So in the process, you eventually get to the step where you go to your next door neighbor and say, "I'm so sorry I backed up my car over your daughter's dog when I was blotto a few weeks ago. I've come to apologize and see what I can do to make amends."

And your neighbor is just as likely to turn to you and give you the easy answer—oh, yes, the easy answer—"Oh, that's okay, the dog was old and she probably didn't see you. She's gotten over it now, you're fine. I'm glad you're getting help." Done! Huge sigh of relief! You don't have to do anything, the apology is accepted! Cross that one off, move on to the next one. That's the easy one; that's the one we want.

And then there's another option, which is really, really harsh, but still easy. That's when your neighbor says, "I never want to see you again, get off my property, don't talk to my family, if I see you anywhere near here I'll call the police and have you arrested." *Slam.*

Oh boy. That's harsh. "I was trying to apologize and make amends," I tell myself. On the other hand, they have reason to be mad at me. So that response is legit. And best of all, I still don't have to do anything except stay away from them. That's another easy one. It's not nice, but it's easy.

The third response is the one we need, and don't want.

"Thank you for coming over to apologize. That was my daughter's therapy dog; she has an anxiety disorder and a learning disability and she hasn't been able to leave the house to go to school since the dog died. Since my wife and I both work full time, we'd like to know if you would have the time to help to locate the new dog of the right temperament to be a therapy dog, and make sure it's the right kind of dog for our daughter, and pay for the training as well. Do you have the time for that?"

So what do you say to that? "Uhhhh . . ."

You can see that a person of limited resources has to get very creative about making amends, and we all have to recognize that sometimes amends are not what we think they are.

But if you are privileged economically, you can say, "I will pay for anything you like. Find an expert, I'll pay. Absolutely, I'll cover it all." Whew. Money does a lot. Money buys things. Still, that's kind of, well, easy.

However, if you do this the right way, then you have to say, "I don't know anything about this. Tell me where to find an expert, I'll find out everything I can, I'll do what I can do. I'll help your daughter find a new dog—I'll bring people here since she can't leave the house, she can meet new dogs, whatever I need to do."

Because that will actually move you toward the third step of being a different person—and that's where almost everyone has the hardest time.

It is so hard to change who we are because we come to these awarenesses of failure and damage as adults, as fully formed people, recognizing, "Oh, oops, there are parts of myself I don't like and need to change." But then we also say, "That's really hard work, and so I think I'll just kind of not do that."

We are created as human, fully human beings, and yes, we all do this, in varying degrees, all the time. Fortunately for us, God loves us for being who we are, and that's why the whole idea of punishment doesn't work. God doesn't punish us for the mistakes we make; God lets us do it to ourselves.

And the act of repentance, the work of repentance, is a kind of self-destruction because when you get to that third stage, and you've undone the person you used to be, and made yourself into a whole new person. And in the Jonah story, guess what all the people of Nineveh are busy doing? They have chosen their own calamity. They have chosen their own overthrow, and so God is not saying, "I'll let them off the hook." God is saying, "I don't have to do anything—they've already done it."

They have chosen to be different people. They have overthrown their bad nature and are moving toward a whole new way of being. And they may not succeed at becoming better humans; they may fall down on it; they may become self-righteous jerks about it in a whole 'nother way. But they're giving it an effort; they're trying. They're rebuilding themselves. That's all the calamity they need. And that's fabulous! That's exactly what we want for Nineveh.

Except for Jonah, who's sitting over here in his little sulk, 'cause he didn't get his schadenfreude. He wants his schadenfreude, he's not gonna go home without it. He's gonna sit here and whine.

And God can only say, "I'm sorry for you, dude. That's not how I roll."

# 25

# Who Is Your Nathan?

**Gary Peluso-Verdend**

Rev. Dr. Gary Peluso-Verdend is the president and associate professor of practical theology at Phillips Theological Seminary in Tulsa, Oklahoma, and the author of *Paying Attention: Focusing Your Congregation on What Matters.* This sermon was preached in the Meinders Chapel at Phillips Seminary on January 31, 2017.

• • •

*2 Samuel 12:1–7a*

Who is your Nathan? Better yet, who are your Nathans? From whom can you learn? From whom can you receive correction? Whom do you allow to hold up a mirror in front of your soul and ask you to see yourself? Moreover, after seeing yourself, might you change based on what someone else enabled you to see?

About 15 years ago, I led a study for the Association of Theological Schools. The study focused on the perspectives students brought to seminary, and how the students judged seminary affected their perspectives. My research colleague and I discovered, not surprisingly, that the students who were open to what seminary offered changed the most. We named that openness the value of suffer-ability. An ancient meaning of "suffer" is to be vulnerable, to be open to change. That meaning is expressed in the hymn verse "if thou but suffer God to guide thee."[1]

The opposite of sufferable would be insufferable. People who are self-righteous are insufferable. Those who are a rule unto themselves, those who do not believe they are in need of forgiveness, are unable to be a human being with others.

It's the nature of humanity to be limited in perspective; we cannot know everything. To be limited is to be human. To act from our limitations and to make mistakes is no sin. In fact, it's when we deny our humanity, it's when we deny our finitude and think we have God's mind that we move over from error into sin, into claiming to be a law unto ourselves.

There is an affinity between a famous biblical story and the science of how our brains work. Recall the interaction between an angry Cain and God, on the one hand, and modern understanding of the brain and mind, on the other hand. In Genesis 4:6–7, Cain is angry because God favored Abel's offering. God asks Cain, "Why are you angry? If you do well, won't you be accepted? And if you do not do well, sin is lurking at your door; its desire is for you, but you must master it." Think about it. In the story, God takes the time to instruct Cain. But Cain still kills Abel. If God speaking to you to "be careful" does not change your behavior, what will?

Why is mastering the impulse to hurt someone so hard? Because the impulse to justify what one wants to do is so strong. Bending reality to justify our interests is not the whole of our nature, but it's in our nature. Human beings are brain-prone to confirm a bias we previously formed or to justify what we want to do or even what we did. This brain bias is another way of saying "sin is lurking at our door, and its desire is for you." The desire to bend reality to suit oneself can be overwhelming.

In the ancient and Renaissance worlds, the image was of a rider (reason) trying to bridle and steer powerful horses (the passions). If reason is strong enough, it can steer the passions, or so the ancients hoped. In the contemporary world, Chip and Dan Heath are credited with the analogy of the rider and the elephant. The elephant is the emotional and unconscious self. The rider represents reason, persuading the elephant and sometimes justifying what the elephant did. The rider can persuade but cannot really steer.[2]

Ben Franklin expresses the elephant rider's role well: "So convenient a thing to be a reasonable creature, since it enables one to find or make a reason for everything one has a mind to do."

This reasonable warping of reality to serve our interests is why I say everyone needs a Nathan. Nathans keep us honest, humble, ethical, and human.

A person in a position of power with no Nathans may be what Jungian therapists call a high-chair tyrant. Imagine the toddler demanding to be fed, fidgeting to get out, throwing to the floor or wall anything they don't like. Now imagine some adult you know who throws tantrums in that chair, doing all those high-chair tyrant things.

Let's look at King David, at his high-chair tyrant moment. What was David thinking? Was he like the disgusting French king played by Mel Brooks in the satire/comedy *History of the World Part I*? The king makes up rules for chess as he wants ("I get three moves to your one!"), his sycophant advisers declare "might makes right," and the king is unfiltered, predatory, and creepy when it comes to sex. After doing all kinds of morally despicable actions and saying morally horrible things, Brooks's king turns to us, the disgusted audience and sneers, "It's good to be the king!"[3]

Is that what David was thinking, "It's good to be the king?" The writer of 2 Samuel actually tells us quite a bit about the king's state of mind, and the moral peril he orchestrated for himself. He was bored (walking back and forth on his roof), he was neglecting duty (in the season when kings go off to war, David sent Joab and stayed in Jerusalem), he lusted (he saw her naked, inquired who she was, and then used his office to send for her), and had sex with her, which by today's standards would most likely have been called rape (first meeting, power differential), and to top it off, he covers a rape and resultant pregnancy by ordering a murder.

In this episode, David is a horrible human being. Not the young man courageously battling the enemy Goliath. Not the one who soothed the anguished Saul with his lyre. Not the politically astute king remembered for centuries as the epitome of a kingship. No, here he is all elephant and his rider, I imagine, made up some excuse for why it was okay to take all the dastardly actions he took. Maybe he reasoned he was the king and no one can tell the king what to do, for if the king does it, it's right.

But David had a Nathan.

Think about David and Nathan's relationship. Imagine being Nathan for the moment. How do you think Nathan prepared for that meeting? Did he get his affairs in order, talk with his attorney, put his wife and children in hiding in case the king would seek to kill them after killing Nathan for speaking truth to power?

Now, consider Nathan's position and strategy. Having access to a powerful person is an excellent position to inhabit. Think about what it might take, in terms of courage for the counselor and trust by the powerful person to be so close to someone and know someone so well that you can appeal both to their moral sensibilities and catch them off-guard so thoroughly that they expose their own vulnerability. Nathan catches David by surprise, and cuts through his self-delusion that what he did was okay.

There is much grace in a good knife. A good test of sharpness is slicing a ripe, tender tomato. Can the knife cut without squishing? That's a good, sharp knife.

Do you know the old phrase "cut to the quick," with "quick" used as the word is used in traditional English versions of the Apostles Creed: "from thence he shall come to judge the quick and the dead"? To be cut to the quick is to be cut in a way that threatens your life, but it might also mean to cut through a self-delusion, a self-serving interest, a story we tell ourselves in a way that allows the reality of what we've done to become obvious to us. Being cut to the quick can mean exposing a deception that led us on unhealthy or even deadly paths.

When Nathan held up that mirror to David about the rich man stealing the beloved lamb from the man who had nothing but that lamb, Nathan's words cut David to the quick.

Sometimes data can cut to the quick, the way that climate change data should, the way that demographic projections that challenge white privilege should. Sometimes a powerful image or story can cut to the quick. Think the fire hoses and dogs turned on civil rights marchers in the 1960s, which sickened white Americans enough that President Johnson knew he had the political will to pass the Civil Rights Act. Recall the photo of the body of the tiny refugee child lying lifeless on a beach that, for a period of time, cut some of our nation's elected leaders to the quick.

There is a verse I love from the hymn "Amazing Grace." Some people don't like the words about saving "a wretch like me." Granted. But I love the phrase "'twas grace that taught my heart to fear, and grace that set me free." Often we think of grace as gentle, healing, a balm, something to soothe a troubled spirit. But, in those places in our souls, in our churches, and in our society that are built on self-interest that excludes others, those places where we have twisted privilege into a birthright, in those places where we degrade others to lift ourselves up, in those places where we get self-righteous, then grace first feels like judgment, but it's grace nonetheless. For, in order to grow as human beings, we cannot be insufferable. We have to be vulnerable to the insight, the correction, the teaching that grace requires if God's grace is to transform our lives.

The Nathans in our lives are gifts, and they are grace. We seminary professors and students often think it's our role to be Nathan to others. No argument. But it's essential that *everyone* with any power suffers at least one Nathan.

---

[1]Georg Neumark, trans. Catherine Winkworth, "If Thou But Suffer God to Guide Thee," public domain.

[2]See the Heath Brothers, "Three Surprises about Change," http://heathbrothers.com/switch-chapter-1/.

[3]Mel Brooks, "It's Good to Be the King," https://www.youtube.com/watch?v=l-2h4XnKZ3g.

# 26

# We Are "Them"

**Jeff Chu**

Jeff Chu is a Brooklyn-based freelance reporter and writer as well as a seminarian at Princeton Theological Seminary. He's the author of *Does Jesus Really Love Me? A Gay Christian's Pilgrimage in Search of God in America.* His work has appeared in such places as *The New York Times Magazine, The Wall Street Journal, The Washington Post,* and *Time.* This sermon was preached at Princeton Theological Seminary on November 30, 2017.

• • •

*Hebrews 6:1-8*

In the spring of 2013, the Christian author Rachel Held Evans resolved to do something different for Lent. Rachel is the author of a *New York Times* best-seller called *A Year of Biblical Womanhood,* in which she tried to follow every biblical regulation for a woman literally—it was part humor, part theological commentary. She has been on a long journey from evangelicalism into the Episcopal Church, from complementarianism to egalitarianism, from social conservatism to a place of bold advocacy for her LGBTQ+ siblings. The public documentation of that journey, much of it on Twitter and Facebook, has stirred enormous vitriol. Multiple people have compared her to Jezebel. She has regularly been told that she's a tool of the devil. She has publicly been declared a non-Christian.

One of the most devastating things about this flood of opposition is that it has come almost entirely from people of faith. Some of the most scathing slams have come from pastors. An author and speaker specializing in Christian apologetics called her a "heretic apostate." Another self-declared "lover of Jesus" said that she was a false teacher inspired by Satan. Someone whose Twitter bio says he is "theologically Barthian" and "I try to be kind on Twitter" wrote to her: "You have no room to judge anyone's theology as yours is truly Satanic."

If you happen to be more conservative than Held Evans, no worries: she's just one tiny example in a river of vitriol that flows both ways.

Self-described progressive Christians just as quickly proof-text, judge, and accuse conservatives of being "anti-Christ." What seems to win the day are sound bites, snark, takedowns, and shade. And what's remarkable is that so much of the sniping is *among* Christians. We are not above the fray; so often, we are right in the midst of it—and not just in the midst of it, but reveling in it. But at what cost? We are seeing some of the toll in our country today. The polarized climate has led to what we might call an epistemological crisis, where, increasingly, truth has quotation marks around it, news is declared fake because it doesn't serve our purposes, and we doubt any information source with which we do not already agree. Our discourse has become toxic.

Yet our merciful God, through passages of scripture like Hebrews 6, reminds us that there is always hope—and always a better word. I acknowledge that Hebrews 6 doesn't seem a natural choice to address these concerns. So many other snippets of scripture talk about gentleness and humility—Paul's stuff about the fruit of the Spirit, for instance, or Jesus's admonition to love one another. But this passage has something to tell us, I think, about the costs of *not* displaying the fruits of the Spirit, of *not* loving one another.

This section of the Letter to the Hebrews is a bridge. In previous chapters, the writer has laid a foundation, dropping historically revered names— Moses and Joshua—and connecting them with Jesus, who has already been introduced as our great high priest, as someone who understands human temptation, as an advocate who is gracious and merciful.

Here, the writer indicates that we're done with the basics. We're going deeper. He's setting up subsequent chapters of Hebrews, which dive more intricately into Jesus's role as our great High Priest and King and what that means for our lives of faith.

Yet this bridge is no mere convenient transition. It's worth standing here and lingering for a bit. There's quite a view from this spot, with important lessons for how we are to relate to one another.

This section of scripture has conventionally (and often) been framed as a dire warning against apostasy. Many centuries of theologians have debated what it means to turn your back on a faith you once claimed and proclaimed, and this passage has been an important part of the discussion. Indeed, it's easy for those of us who find ourselves still in the church to dismiss its relevance to us. We shouldn't.

I understand why we shy away. Verse six, for instance, says that apostates "are crucifying again the Son of God and are holding him up to contempt." Who among us wants to be involved in the re-crucifixion of Christ?

I understand, too, why this passage has so often been used as a bludgeon against "them." Those people who grew up in church and no longer go. Those people who, in the language of my upbringing, "have walked away from the Lord" and "haven't made room for Jesus in their hearts." Those people who make the faith look bad. Those people who fail to behave in Christ-like ways. Those people who tweet unwisely and lash out at people in Facebook comments. Those people. Those apostates. We do not want to see ourselves as *"them."*

Here's the ugly truth: *we are "them."*

What the NRSV translates as "holding Jesus up to contempt" can be more literally translated as "subjecting Christ to open and public shaming."

*We are "them."* Because we apostatize all the time, if apostasy means making something other than Jesus primary in our lives and if apostasy means putting ourselves in the place of judge of others. We apostatize all the time, tweeting or posting Facebook statuses or comments in pettiness or jealousy or selfish ambition, craving likes and retweets with clever cruelness or humor at someone else's expense. We apostatize all the time—daily and even more than that, both privately and publicly, if it means saying something that might bring Christ into disrepute in a twisted formula of guilt by association.

*We are "them."*

So thank God for the delete button—and yet, there is much more hope than that. We see that hope tucked neatly amid the warning, with, for instance, that seemingly passing allusion in verse five to "the powers of the age to come." There's a tantalizing hint of the inbreaking of God into this beautiful yet broken world—and who would dare argue that those divine powers could be limited by our human failures?

*We are "them."*

Yet we receive hope too in the agricultural portrait at the end of the passage, an echo of Jesus's rurally minded parables. The writer paints a picture of a piece of land and two possible harvests. One is a blessed season, producing crops that feed and nourish. The other has us thinking that the land is "on the verge of being cursed." All that springs up are thorns and thistles, vexation and pain.

Amid this bleak picture, I think the writer intentionally plants a seed of hope. The land of thorns and thistles, the writer says, is "on the verge of being cursed." It is not cursed now—not just yet. All is not lost. God isn't done yet. There is still hope here. This side of kingdom come, there's always hope, even in seemingly barren terrain, even in parched soil, even on Twitter.

Six years ago, I made one of my most difficult reporting trips—as a journalist, as a Christian, as someone who is gay. I was in the midst of a project seeking to understand how America's Christians claim to worship the same God, the same Jesus, yet hold radically, sometimes violently, different views on sexuality. Because I wanted to do a thorough job as a journalist and because I am a slight masochist, I traveled to Topeka, Kansas, to Westboro Baptist Church, the congregation most famous for its "God Hates Fags" signs. They have contributed immensely to the coarseness of the debate about homosexuality and the church—and through their media presence, they've achieved outsize influence.

One morning, I went to see them picketing outside a Topeka church, holding their toxic signs. There, I met a six-year-old boy named Ben. He told me about his fears of going to school and about his sadness that his school, he had heard, didn't have a trampoline like his backyard did. The whole time we talked, he was holding a sign that read, "F\*\*gs Doom Nations."

I didn't have it in my heart to be angry at Ben, to hate Ben, to shame this adorable 6-year-old boy on Twitter or Facebook, as sad as his sign made me. And I wondered: At what point do I get to shame him or hate him?

By my presence, I was opposing the message on that sign. With my very person, I was protesting. With my body, I was defying the hateful words. But part of me wanted more: to exact vengeance, to shame him, to shame them. But . . .

*We are "them."*

To be honest, I never could settle on an age at which the grace that I believe in, the hope expressed even in a land on the verge of being cursed, no longer applied to Ben. And about 18 months after that visit, I got a call from another church member, Megan Phelps-Roper, who was one of the most influential, because she spearheaded Westboro's social-media efforts.

Megan was crying. She had left the church.

I'd stayed in touch with her a bit, because she'd seemed nice. She had puzzled over why it was that I was so different from the kind of gay person she'd been taught that all gay people are. She had wrestled with why others she encountered, both in person and online, didn't seem like the demons that she'd been taught they were.

Has most of the rest of the world written Westboro off as land not worth our attention and care, as worth nothing but thistles and thorns, brutal signs and ugly vulgarity? And who else do we write off like this, as beyond hope?

Yet can you see the hope even in the very last words of verse eight, where it says that the end of this land is to be burned over? In fact, even that end has hope—hope through the new start that can come with purifying fire, hope through the fertility that ash can produce, hope that new life can come even through death.

We have a new way to understand this agricultural metaphor here at Princeton Seminary: the Farminary, the seminary's 21-acre farm. For years, it was a sod farm. Sod farming is one of the most debilitating, earth-abusing forms of farming there is. With every harvest, you take not just the new grass but also the topsoil beneath it. Eventually, the land is nearly barren, stripped of nutrients.

When Nate Stucky started the Farminary, the soil was so devoid of goodness that one might even say it was "on the verge of being cursed." But through composting, Stucky is nursing the soil back to health. In composting, death produces new life. With the help of worms and grubs and the heat of the sun, the end of a season for an apple or a squash or autumn leaves feeds the beginning of a new season for a new crop. Knit into God's creation, we see this cycle of life and death and resurrection. Even in midwinter, when so much outside looks like death, it bears the promise of life.

Friends, the writer of Hebrews seems to understand that deep complexity in our humanity, calling us to our best selves even while acknowledging our worst primal instincts. Indeed, in the death of those instincts, in being called out of that life, we discover the new life of our best selves. We know we will fail. We know we will tarnish God's good name. Yet Jesus keeps calling us toward spiritual maturity, toward the perfection that can only come in and through Him, toward love. And even amid our stumbles and setbacks, our emotional autumns and our spiritual winters, our merciful God reminds us that there is always hope.

As we approach each other in these turbulent times, and especially through the often-distorted lenses of social media and with the distance of technology, we are called to a pursuit of maturity and perfection in our discourse. Not showy, preening, peacock-like perfection, in which we display what we think are our personal glories, but perfection in imitation of Christ—in humility, in service, in companionship, in grace, in love.

Hebrews 6 gives us a sense of the stakes, and it returns us to the long-term reality that our choices reflect on the reputation of the Jesus who has loved us and claimed us as His own. Here, we begin to understand how our actions and reactions produce ripples—or is it too often, rips and tears?—in our relationships with one another and with God. How countercultural it would be if we tweeted at one another in encouragement and love. How powerful it might be if we offered one another the gift of vulnerability and care. How bold it would be if we opted out of the ways of this world and instead created something beautiful amid the ugliness.

Here's what Rachel Held Evans decided to do with her hate mail: She printed out the electronic slams and slights. She stacked them up with all that had come via the old-fashioned postal service. And she started to fold them into origami, into swans and sailboats, foxes and flowers. "It felt a little awkward at first," she writes, "but as I moved my fingers across those painful words, folding them into one another to make wings, then a neck, then a crooked little beak, healing tears fell, and I let my fingers pray."[1]

*We are "them."*

And yet Jesus loves us so much. He is the one who has folded us and our ugliness into new life forms and new beauty. What might it mean to look at others and always see hope of redemption? What might it mean to walk through the world with the humble posture of a recipient of lavish grace? What might it mean to understand that God's love for you doesn't reduce, not even one bit, the love God has for anyone else? What might it mean to recognize that, even having received these gorgeous gifts, still we fail?

Still, we proclaim the name of the Christ who loves us so much—and then we re-crucify him all over. And yet, and yet, and yet, there his arms are, still open wide, still ready to receive and embrace us again.

———————

[1]Rachel Held Evans, "What I learned turning my hate mail into origami," https://rachelheldevans.com/blog/what-i-learned-turning-my-hate-mail-into-origami.

# 27

# Good News vs. Fake News

---

**Susan Russell**

Rev. Susan Russell serves as a senior associate rector at All Saints Church in Pasadena, California, where this sermon was preached on July 13, 2017. She is the past president of Integrity (the Episcopal LGBTQ+ caucus) and founding member of the Human Rights Commission's Faith and Religion Council. The purpose of this sermon, she notes, is to reflect on how to persist in resisting evil without becoming the evil we deplore.

· · ·

*Matthew 13:31–33; 44–52*

*"Let there be peace among us, and let us not be instruments of our own or others' oppression. Amen."*

Some of you will remember this prayer—the one I've come to think of as the Gospel According to Barbara. They are the words Bishop Barbara Harris—the first woman bishop in the Anglican Communion—has used to begin every sermon I've ever heard her preach. They are also the words that have become my own mantra to stay focused as an active member of The Resistance.

And boy have they been getting a workout over these last days, weeks, and months.

In our Collect this morning we prayed that we might: "so pass through things temporal, that we lose not the things eternal."

It's the same prayer we pray absolutely every year at this point in the lectionary cycle; yet it's arguable that in this particular year the tsunami of the 24-hour news cycle has made holding on to those "things eternal" more of a challenge than many of us can ever remember.

And that is why gathering together is such a critically important part of our resistance. We come together as community to pray, reflect, and recharge—to remember who we are and whose we are. We come together not to escape "things temporal" but in order to engage them in the service of the eternal values of love, justice, and compassion.

And then we go out—refueled and refreshed by the bread and wine made holy. We go out to love, serve, challenge—and resist—for another week.

It's who we are as All Saints Church. It's part of our DNA.

A few weeks ago I was making my way to the chapel for Noon Eucharist and one of the memorial plaques caught my eye. Now, next Tuesday will be the 16th anniversary of my first day of work here at All Saints Church. So it's fair to say I have walked by that memorial plaque literally hundreds of times.

But for some reason—that quiet weekday morning in an empty church—it tapped on my shoulder and demanded my attention. It reads:

In affectionate memory of Julia Adele Meeker.

A consecrated member of this parish

rich in good works for all peoples.

"She fought the good fight

and kept the faith."

1861–1930

Julia Adele Meeker was born the year that the Civil War tore our nation apart and died the year after the Wall Street crash threw it into the Great Depression—with the First World War thrown in between. I can't even imagine the troubles she saw—the challenges she faced—the evils she resisted. And yet what we know is at the end of her life what the community who loved her wanted us to know about her was that she was rich in good works for all peoples . . . and that she fought the good fight.

One of my teachers and mentors is historian Fredrica Harris Thompsett. She taught us that the reason we learn our history is to get a running start on our future. And so as we gather this morning to be refueled and refreshed for the challenges ahead of us, it bears remembering our history.

It bears knowing that we stand on the shoulders of all those who have gone before us—those known and unknown to us—who (like Julia Adele Meeker) fought the good fight. And to recognize that the fight we fight—the resistance in which we engage—the struggle that continues—is not just an historic one. It's a cosmic one.

It's the fight between nothing less than good and evil. It's the cosmic struggle between the good news of love, justice, and inclusion and the fake news of fear, judgment, and discrimination.

Now, the term may have been coined in the last election cycle but "fake news" has always been around. It's as ancient as the mythological story of the serpent in the Garden telling the first humans they didn't need God—they could do it themselves if they just ate from that forbidden tree.

It's woven into the narrative of our spiritual family album in story after story after story as we chose domination over collaboration; chose our own way over God's way; chose fear over faith. And it was part of this morning's reading from the Hebrew scriptures when Solomon—given the gift of whatever he might ask of God—asked for discernment between good and evil.

Cosmic fake news manifests itself in what theologian Walter Wink described as "the domination system"—which operates according to the myth of redemptive violence, entrapping us all in the amazingly self-destructive dynamic of violence responding with violence to violence and on and on.[1]

When I discovered Walter Wink's work in seminary I discovered a powerful tool to understand both the depth of our culture's commitment to the way of violence and the power of the gospel as a viable alternative to that way of violence: of the power of the good news of love to ultimately triumph over the ongoing struggle to defeat the fake news of domination. The struggle continues; *la lucha continua*.

A critical part of that struggle is to refuse to become the evil we deplore; to bear witness to the truth that resistance and reconciliation are not mutually exclusive. We put into action the truth that we can be both resisters and reconcilers every time we offer this blessing: "And the blessing of God Almighty be with you—those you love, serve, challenge and resist—this day and always."

We're lovers and servers and challengers and—yes—resisters. And yet even as we resist we ask God's blessing on those we resist.

Because the good fight we are fighting is on behalf of the good news of the God who loved us enough to become one of us in the person of Jesus. And the Jesus we follow is the one who will not rest until there is not a single stranger left at the gate.

I'd like to ask you to close your eyes. Picture the person you would most *not* want to be in heaven with. Have you got someone? Well, Jesus won't rest until that person is inside the gate, gathered into the loving embrace of the kingdom of love, justice, and compassion. That is the Jesus we follow.

Today's gospel reading from the 13th chapter of Matthew is a little bit like all of the best outtakes that were left on the cutting room floor pulled together so they don't get lost in the annals of time:

The kingdom is like a mustard seed . . .
The kingdom is like yeast in a loaf of bread . . .
The kingdom is like a treasure . . .
The kingdom is like a pearl of great price . . .
The kingdom is like a net cast into the sea . . .

Jesus had as many parables as there were people to hear them because there is no "one-size-fits-all" story about the kingdom of God. For the kingdom of God is as deep and as wide and as abundant as the infinite love of God.

The good news we've staked our lives on is that we can resist to our last breath—blog post, tweet, email, protest, march, and petition—the actions of those who participate in the oppressive domination systems that surround us, while at the same time refusing to let the "fake news" that they are anything less than beloved children of God win out over the good news that God loves us all beyond our wildest imaginings.

As Walter Wink writes, "Evil can be opposed without being mirrored. Oppressors can be resisted without being emulated. Enemies can be neutralized without being destroyed."[2] We can fight the good fight without losing sight of the good news in the process.

Our baptismal promise to respect the dignity of every human being requires us to stand up and speak out when the dignity of any member of the human family is threatened. Just last week we stood in solidarity with members of the transgender community who once again found themselves being used as sacrificial lambs on the altar of partisan politics. The unconscionable attack by the current administration on the fitness of transgender Americans to serve in the military was not only unwarranted—it was antithetical to our core values as Americans and as Christians. As our brilliant friend Susan Thistlethwaite wrote:

> Transgender Americans do not "weaken" the military or the country. The profound truth of the American experiment, when we are living up to it, is that we are much, much stronger as a people when all are treated equally and have equal rights. Blaming and shaming transgender people is not only a betrayal of our national political aspirations to "all" being "created equal," it is a betrayal of deeply held religious values.[3]

At All Saints Church we will continue to stand with and for all those on the margins. We stand with all those in danger of losing health care, with anyone being profiled because of their race or their religion, with neighbors under threat of deportation, with refugees seeking a safe haven and with Dreamers seeking an education. We will challenge those who applaud excessive force by law enforcement officers and those who threaten to undermine equal protection for LGBTQ+ Americans. We refuse to choose between competing oppressions; instead we will stand together and resist any and all assaults on the dignity, the safety, and the humanity of any and all of God's beloved human family.

And we will not allow ourselves to be either distracted or discouraged as we continue to live out All Saints' DNA-deep commitment to turn the human race into the human family—a commitment that fuels our resistance, sustains us in the struggle, and inspires our vision for a kingdom come on earth as it is in heaven that includes absolutely everyone.

Full stop. No exceptions. Period.

One of the handful of biblical citations I carry around in my back pocket at all times is John 8:32, "the truth will make you free." And the truth is that Jesus didn't come to make people comfortable; Jesus came to tell the truth about the good news of God's inclusive love available to absolutely everybody and to debunk the fake news that some people are more loved, more saved, or more worthy.

If Jesus's goal was to make people comfortable then there would've been no cross and there would've been no resurrection and we wouldn't be here over two thousand years later still fighting the good fight.

Many years ago our Rector Emeritus, George Regas, challenged us to live out the prophetic gospel by "setting audacious goals and celebrating incremental victories."

This morning we are still celebrating the incremental victory that came in the wee hours of Friday morning: the defeat of the latest effort to take health care away from millions of Americans. It was an incremental victory (make no mistake about it: we know that battle is far from over). And yet against a lot of odds the combined voices of women and men over days and weeks and months—in the streets and on the phones and at town hall meetings and in the halls of Congress—including my mother-in-law who called her senator so often that when she called the intern answered, "Good morning, Mrs. Hall. What can we do for you today?" Together we fought the good fight—like our sister Julia Adele Meeker—and proved once again that together we can make a difference for "all peoples."

In a few moments we'll again come together around this table—not to escape "things temporal" but to engage them in the service of the eternal values of love, justice, and compassion. And then we will ask God to send us out—refueled and refreshed once again by the bread and wine made holy—to love, serve, challenge—and resist—for another week.

Let there be peace among us, and let us not be instruments of our own or others' oppression. Amen.

---

[1]See Walter Wink, *The Powers That Be* (New York: Doubleday, 1998).
[2]Ibid., 111.
[3]Susan Thistlethwaite, "Manufacturing Resentment: Trump Targets Transgender Americans in Military," *The Huffington Post*, July 26, 2017, https://www. huffingtonpost.com/entry/manufacturing-resentment-trump-targets-transgender_ us_5978c976e4b01cf1c4bb74e2.

# 28

# The End of Beastly Empire

**Brian Zahnd**

Rev. Brian Zahnd is the author of numerous books including, most recently, *Sinners in the Hands of a Loving God* and *A Farewell to Mars*. He's also founder and lead pastor of Word of Life Church, a nondenominational congregation in St. Joseph, Missouri. This sermon was preached at Word of Life on October 26, 2014, as part of the series, "Exile: Living as the People of God in a Modern Day Babylon." [Editor's note: this is an edited transcript produced from an audio recording; some phrases and quotes are paraphrased from the original.[1]]

• • •

*Daniel 7*

The book of Daniel is about the Jewish people learning to live as the people of God in the midst of a pagan empire. The tension is that you don't want to get killed by the empire, but you don't want to compromise with it either. Which is pretty tricky to do. How do you walk the tightrope between engaged citizenship and covenant faithfulness? It's similar to the tension in the book of Revelation, which is about first-century Christians learning how to be faithful in the midst of Roman Empire. Both Daniel and Revelation speak to us today about how to be the people of God in the midst of a modern-day Babylon. They give us strategies to help us resist losing our baptismal identity under the pressure of empire. When someone is baptized it means they've been formally received into the kingdom of Christ. Henceforth and forevermore, their primary allegiance is to Jesus, whom we confess is Lord.

There have been empires throughout history. Empires are rich, powerful nations that believe they have a divine right to rule other nations as part of their "manifest destiny." The problem with these empires is that they always end up in conflict with the desires of God, primarily because only Christ is given the divine right to rule. Empires inevitably become inhumane and, thus, anti-Christ. Because whatever is antihuman is anti-Christ.

As followers of Jesus, and as citizens of the nation with the world's largest economy and most powerful military, we face the same kinds of challenges as these Jewish exiles and early Christians. American Christians have to learn how to live like Jewish exiles and early Christians in the midst of empire. We have to live in the tension between engaged, responsible citizenship, and, at the same time, covenant faithfulness springing from our baptismal identity.

In today's passage of scripture, Daniel is dreaming at night and he sees the ocean. It's a stormy night; the ocean is stirred up. As modern people, we've fallen in love with the ocean. We're enamored with it. But that's not the way it was with the ancients. The ancients saw the sea as dark and foreboding, filled with monsters; you never know what might come up out of the sea. It became a metaphor for chaos, anxiety, and the wellspring of evil. In Daniel's dream, the dark sea was stirred up by the four winds. And then, one after another, four beasts came out of the sea. These beasts are malevolent. They stalk across the land. In their wake they leave destruction and suffering. They emerged from the sea in the form of a lion, bear, leopard, and monster. Most popular interpreters identify them as symbols of empire: Babylon, Persia, Greece, and Rome. Or Assyria, Babylon, Persia, and Greece (it depends on when people think Daniel was written). Either way, the symbolism stands for empire. To understand this, imagine how history might be told from the vantage point of enslaved Africans, or Native Americans. They might say something like, "Well it was the Portuguese that came first. They were like a lion, devouring everything. Then came the Spanish, like a bear. Then the Dutch, springing on us like a leopard. And then the English, worst of all. They were like a monster."

So the first part of Daniel's dream is a summation of world history, of one empire after another asserting its will. And those who suffer are always the oppressed people. The poor people. The people that don't have conventional power. They get trampled underfoot by what feels like a lion, bear, leopard, or monster.

After describing the parade of beastly empire, Daniel sees a court up in the heavens. There's a great gathering of people along with one who sits upon the throne as the Ancient One, or the Ancient of Days. His clothing is white as light; his hair is white as wool. His throne is made of fire. It is an image of God. Daniel turns from prose to poetry to describe this part of his dream:

As I watched in the night visions,
I saw one like a human being
    coming with the clouds of heaven.
And he came to the Ancient One
    and was presented before him.
To him was given dominion

and glory and kingship,
that all peoples, nations, and languages
    should serve him.
His dominion is an everlasting dominion
    that shall not pass away,
and his kingship is one
    that shall never be destroyed. (7:13–14)

When one observes the parade of beastly empires that always leave oppression in their wake, one can easily despair and think, "Well, this is just the way it is. This is the way it's always going to be. The strong press the weak; it's how it is." But the prophet sees another picture. He sees "one like a human being," coming with the clouds of heaven, being presented to the Ancient of Days. And the Ancient of Days gives to this human being (also rendered as the Son of Man), dominion over all languages and tribes and tongues. And unlike these other beastly empires that come and go, this one is going to come and stay. It's not going to fall. And the difference is that it's not beastly, it's human. It's not beastly, it's humane. The poor and the afflicted and the suffering will flourish under the reign of this human, or humane, empire.

That's the dream that Daniel has, and the little poem he writes about it. It's also a thing called the gospel. *This is the gospel.* The hope that beastly empire will come to an end and that a humane empire, benefitting the poor and oppressed, will come from heaven. Because God acts on behalf of humanity, and appoints a Son of Man to have authority over all of the nations, peoples, tribes, and tongues. It's the vision that the kingdom, or empire, of God, or of heaven, is going to come. And this—watch how this all fits together now—this is the primary thing that Jesus talked about—by far. In all of his sermons, in all of his parables, he's talking about one thing: the kingdom of God. He's talking about the kingdom that comes from heaven. And whereas Jesus is the messiah, he hardly ever calls himself messiah. Instead, what does Jesus call himself more than 80 times? The Son of Man. And who is the Son of Man? It's a direct reference to the human one from Daniel 7.

In the New Testament we encounter the word *gospel*, which means good news. However, it's not just good news—it's good news announced by the king, from a royal source. This word is inherited from Hebrew scripture, especially the book of Isaiah, where it's used five times. Early in Jesus's ministry, he stood up in his hometown synagogue and quoted Isaiah:

The Spirit of the Lord is upon me,
    because he has anointed me
    to bring good news to the poor.
He has sent me to proclaim release to the captives

and recovery of sight to the blind,
      to let the oppressed go free,
to proclaim the year of the Lord's favour. (Luke 4:18–19)

Jesus was saying, "This is my job description. Remember all that stuff you read about in Isaiah 61, when God will break into history and establish God's rule, and those who benefit are the poor, the oppressed, and the marginalized? Well, I'm the one that's bringing that to pass now." It's a daring claim, but it's what Jesus says.

So, what is the gospel? According to the prophets, who then pass it on to the apostles, the gospel is the good news that the messiah brings the rule of God to this world—replacing empire, bringing peace, and liberating the poor and oppressed. That's the good news. That's the gospel.

But there's something modern readers may not know. When Jesus was born, the world already had a savior. (Listen to me carefully.) When Jesus was born, the world already had a savior. The world already had a gospel. The world had a savior who had a title—it was on all the coins in all the realm. The name for the Savior of the World, the Prince of Peace, the Son of God, was . . . *Augustus Caesar.* All of the coins of the day—those were the billboards of the day—had the image of Caesar Augustus, with various accompanying titles like Savior of the World, Son of God, and Prince of Peace. And the gospel was the Pax Romana—the peace of Rome. Which was a bit of propaganda, to say the least.

You see, empire always announces itself as gospel. Empire always calls itself the last, best hope of earth. It speaks as a lamb, but in the end it's always a beast. It's always a beast because its gospel is always violent. It brings peace by killing and prosperity by oppression, and all violent empires of the world are ultimately beastly.

As Christians, we are not called to worship the beast of empire—even if one views some empires as being kinder, gentler beasts than others. No. We are those who worship and confess Jesus Christ as Lord. Sometimes that confession gets reduced to a nice, germane, safe, antiseptic, religious statement that usually produces little more than a yawn. But please understand: in its original formulation and context, proclaiming "Jesus is Lord" was deeply subversive—because the gospel of the empire was "Caesar is Lord."

Who was Jesus? He was a Jewish guy who preached parables and proclaimed the kingdom of God and the empire killed him. But guess what? On the third day God raised him. And he is reigning and ruling over the nations right now. The empire would say, "Well, it doesn't look like it." But the Christian would say, "Well, 'we walk by faith and not by sight' (2 Cor. 5:7). We believe this."

And the Roman Empire? It's gone. The Roman Empire has been swept away into the dustbin of history. You can read about it in history books, but it's gone. And yet this kingdom of Christ, that always appears to be failing, always appears to be on the brink of disaster, somehow it's never swept away, it remains.

Why were the early Christians persecuted? It wasn't for telling people how to go to heaven when they die. The Roman Empire would say, "We don't care where you go when you die. Go to heaven? Go to hell? We don't care. If that's your gospel—how to go to heaven when you die—we don't care. Knock yourself out." But that is not what they were doing. They weren't simply telling people how to go to heaven when they die; they were announcing that Jesus Christ is Lord, and *Caesar is not*. The beastly empire tried to destroy him, but God vindicated him in resurrection. He ascended into the clouds, and he sits at the right hand of God. He is judging the nations even now, and we are those seeking to live under his humane rule, here and now.

Jesus brings the peace of God, the empire doesn't. (The Pax Romana, the peace of Rome, is an oxymoron.) The kingdom of heaven, the kingdom of God, the kingdom of Christ comes quietly like seed being sown, like crops as they grow, like a long walk home, like a feast where everyone is welcome. And we enter that kingdom by faith and baptism. At the center of that kingdom is a table. For Jesus is going to change the world not on a battlefield but at a table.

People ask, "Where is the kingdom of God?" It's right here. It's right at this table, where everyone is invited to this place of radical equality. There's neither male nor female, slave nor free, Jew nor Gentile, Democrat nor Republican, rich nor poor. All of these divisions fade away at this table. The gospel makes us rethink everything from the top. You've got to rethink everything or you won't perceive this kingdom. Because it comes so differently than what we're used to. It doesn't come up out of the sea like a beast and announce itself with great violence and destruction. It grows like seed; it's like bread that's rising. It's like a woman sweeping her house; "Oh, there's that lost coin." It's like a long-lost son that has a change of heart and he comes home, and he finds a feast. That's the kingdom of Christ. That's how it comes. It's not beastly; it's humane. That's why we long for it; that's why we celebrate it; that's why we welcome it. Here, now, and forever, Jesus is Lord.

[1]The full sermon can be heard in its entirety on Word of Life's website, http://wolc.com/watch--listen/sermon-archives/the-end-of-beastly-empire/.

# 29

# Take Me to the River

**Cassandra Gould**

Rev. Dr. Cassandra Gould is the senior pastor of Quinn Chapel A.M.E. Church, the oldest entity in Jefferson City, Missouri, to be started by people of color. She also serves as the executive director of Missouri Faith Voices, a nonprofit network striving for economic dignity and race equity. She is the religious affairs director for Missouri's NAACP conference and has been a lead clergy member helping to organize numerous protests in response to the shooting death of Michael Brown in Ferguson, Missouri. A version of this sermon was originally preached at the United Methodist Women's social justice conference on November 12, 2016, just a few days after the general election.

• • •

*Psalm 46; Luke 3:1–20*

When excavating this text one is forced to utilize historical criticism. The text opens with historical references that suggest the setting of the narrative was in a particular year under a specific kingship and gubernatorial reign, sometime right before the year 30 CE. Tiberius had succeeded his stepfather Augustus, the founder of the Roman Empire (talk about getting the keys to the city!). Herod is the king, Pilate is the governor, and they have some other relatives who are mayors in nearby cities. They were known for their lavish parties and excessive extravagances; they craved power and wealth and believed it was their divine right to hoard it, even at the expense of others.

The gospels invite us to juxtapose all of this with the figure of John the Baptist, who (if we recall Matthew's description) didn't wear royal garments, but clothes made of camel's hair. He didn't eat the royal food or drink the royal wine, but ate locusts and wild honey. It's an immediate image of resistance, with the gospels telling us right away that those who come in the name of the Lord aren't in the business of mirroring the empire. John was Elizabeth and Zechariah's baby, the cousin of Jesus; he had been in close proximity to the prophetic since he was in his mother's womb. He was a figure of protest, showing up at the very beginning of the New Testament.

Back in the year 30, a line had been drawn by the Roman Empire that made John the Baptist, and later Jesus, put their ministries, their witness, and their bodies on the line. It is often on that line—with the cliff behind us and the empire in front of us—that our minds become liberated enough—like John the Baptist's—to allow the word of God to come to us.

Are our minds liberated enough to hear the word of God for today? Perhaps from those whose bodies are on the line now, with the cliff behind them and the empire in front of them?

Can we hear the tone of the weary throats of young people crying in the only language that is empowering to them, the language of protest, proclaimed in the only sanctuary they feel safe in, the streets?

Can we hear them singing hymns, perfectly syncopated where the strong beats become weak and the weak beats become strong?

Can we hear them in Ferguson, saying "Hands up don't shoot!"?

Can we hear them in New York, after the death of Eric Garner, saying "I can't breathe"?

Can we hear the voices crying out since the election?

Can we hear the cries of women, the disabled, the young, and the elderly? Can we hear the cries of black, queer, and poor working whites? Can we hear the cries of Native Americans at Standing Rock and of Latinx friends and neighbors waiting to see which side of the wall they will end up on?

The figure of John the Baptist reminds us that in times of great difficulty and uncertainty, a word from the Lord comes to those with ears to hear. And if we recall the context of John's ministry, in which his life was on the line along with the lives of many others, this means that for us to be ready to hear a word from the Lord today we must be willing to live out our call in close proximity to both *hell and hope*. John the Baptist stayed near enough to the brood of vipers to call them out, as well as to those who felt lost and forgotten and needed to be called in. Justice requires proximity to others, and long distance relationships don't work. Justice is built on relationship reciprocation. We need to be in relationship with others so that—in the words of scholar and theologian Tex Sample—we are able to "people our mind." When we hear of injustice, we should know someone whose story that is by name. We must be close enough to the pain to hear, see, feel, touch, and taste the reality of what is going on in the hearts and homes of our neighbors, especially those society has deemed as the "least of these." We must not be so dislocated by our education, our indulgences in capitalism, nor by our religious rigors, regalia, and rites that we can't hear the cries of our LGBTQ+, black, brown, Asian, and Native American neighbors—or even our neighbors who think their vote on Tuesday was an act of "making America great again."

I'm reminded of the late Dr. Vincent Harding's image of a river. He used the metaphor of a river in relation to the struggle for justice, describing the currents of a river in terms of its

> long, continuous movement . . . sometimes powerful, tumultuous, and roiling with life; at other times meandering and turgid, covered with the ice and snow of seemingly endless winters, all too often even streaked and running with blood. . . . [I]t is possible to recognize that we are indeed the river, and at the same time the river is more than us—generations more, millions more. Through such an opening we may sense that the river of black struggle is people, but it is also the hope, the movement, the transformative power that humans create and that create them, us, and makes them, us, new persons.[1]

The psalmist also speaks of a river—the river of God, where we are restored and renewed. As we read in Psalm 46:

God is our refuge and strength,
>     a very present help in trouble.
Therefore we will not fear, though the earth should change,
>     though the mountains shake in the heart of the sea;
though its waters roar and foam,
>     though the mountains tremble with its tumult.
There is a river whose streams make glad the city of God,
>     the holy habitation of the Most High.
God is in the midst of the city; it shall not be moved;
>     God will help it when the morning dawns.
The nations are in an uproar, the kingdoms totter;
>     he utters his voice, the earth melts.
The Lord of hosts is with us;
>     the God of Jacob is our refuge.
Come, behold the works of the Lord;
>     see what desolations he has brought on the earth.
He makes wars cease to the end of the earth;
>     he breaks the bow, and shatters the spear;
>     he burns the shields with fire.
'Be still, and know that I am God!
>     I am exalted among the nations,
>     I am exalted in the earth.'
The Lord of hosts is with us;
>     the God of Jacob is our refuge.

In times like these—somewhere between hell and hope—we must go to the river that gives life; that creates life; that restores life. Like the river, the struggle for justice can be long and tumultuous; justice requires perseverance and persistence. John the Baptist stayed the course even until death; he put his body on the line and it was an act of liberation.

If we too listen for a word from the Lord today, if we too live our lives in close proximity to hell and hope, if we too join our lives to the long and tumultuous struggle for justice, then we too will go where lives are on the line today, *we will go to the river of justice.*

As I listen for a word from the Lord, I can hear the voices of Black Lives Matter activists reminding us that black bodies have to have value somewhere other than in prison and on the streets of our cities—*we will go to the river of justice with them.*

I can hear the voices of those who are sometimes called the "mothers of the movement": Lucia McBath (Jordan Davis's mother), Lezley McSpadden (Michael Brown's mother), Geneva Reed-Veal (Sandra Bland's mother)—*we will go to the river of justice with them.*

I can hear the voices of our enslaved ancestors who are still saying to the church—not just to the black church but to the church universal— "don't let our living through the belly of ships in the Atlantic ocean and our dying on plantations in this country be in vain." *We will go to the river of justice with them.*

I can hear the groans and fears of LGBTQ+ people, amplified all the more after Tuesday's election. They are crying out on Twitter, the only pulpit in which they are welcome. *We will go to the river of justice with them.*

I can hear the cry of Latinx children wondering how long it will be before their mothers and fathers are deported. *We will go to the river of justice with them.*

I can hear the pain and burden of women wailing at the news that last Tuesday a proclamation was signed that indicated it's okay to grab women in places we dare not mention. *We will go to the river of justice with them.*

For Jesus is in that river, justice is in that river, healing is in that river. *We will go to the river together,* and "all flesh shall see the salvation of God" (Lk. 3:6).

---

[1]Vincent Harding, *There Is a River: The Black Struggle for Freedom in America* (Orlando: Harcourt Brace and Company, 1981), xix.

# 30

# The Gospel of Resistance

**Sarah Trone Garriott**

Rev. Sarah Trone Garriott is the coordinator of interfaith engagement at the Des Moines Area Religious Council. She formerly served as associate pastor of Faith Lutheran Church in Clive, Iowa, where this sermon was preached on November 28, 2016. This was the first sermon she preached following the general election. The manuscript is reproduced in the style that Rev. Trone Garriott uses every time she preaches—to guide phrasing and emphasis.

. . .

*Matthew 24:36–44*

Before I became a pastor,
before I even thought about
becoming one,

I served as an AmeriCorps VISTA volunteer
in Gallup, New Mexico.

I was organizing a conference
for faith leaders
on the issue of domestic violence,

an incredibly commonplace
and deadly threat
to women and children
of every background,
every social standing, every faith.

Between 2001 and 2012
6,488 American soldiers
were killed in
Iraq and Afghanistan.

During that same time
the number of American women
killed
by current or ex-partners,
was twice that number.

But most people have no idea.
Because, this is a problem often hidden
in plain sight.

Ignored, not discussed.

I approached one of the local pastors
about taking part in the planning of
this conference,

and this is what he said to me:

Why would I
want to get involved in that?

People don't want to hear about
that in church.
Church is where people dress up,
show up in their best behavior.

People don't want to bring
their problems to church.

• • •

The Gospel of Matthew was written
in the year 85,
about a decade
after the Roman army destroyed
the temple in Jerusalem.

About two or even three generations,
after the crucifixion of Jesus.

It may be hard for us to relate
to how devastating this was

for the Jewish people
to see the place where God lived,
destroyed.

To see the center of their world,
the axis around which everything revolved,
obliterated.

Today, two thousand years later,
many still gather to weep,
at the one remaining wall of the temple.

But people have a strong desire to
get back to normal,
to find a way to be fine—

—even when everything
all around them is not.

And so for the Jewish community
anything that was different,
challenging,

anything that seemed to threaten
the survival of their faith,

anything that would attract
the brutal anger of the Roman Empire,
had to go.

And so,
the Jewish followers of Jesus,
found themselves being rejected
by their families,
shut out of the synagogues,

they felt disconnected from the story of God's promise to Abraham.

And the years kept passing,
and Jesus had not returned,
and the Jewish followers of Jesus
were trying to figure out how to keep going,
in the face of things
—that were so hard.

There was so much pressure on them
from their Jewish brothers and sisters,
from the Roman government,
to just fit in,
to just be quiet,
to just stop causing trouble.

And they too,
wanted so much for life
to go back to being normal.

And this is the situation
for which this Word, this gospel,
is written.

• • •

The problem in the days of Noah
described here
is not
worshipping golden calves,
or engaging in some horrible, despicable, sinful behavior.

The problem here is that people
have placed too much emphasis
on the cares and tasks of ordinary life.
All their attention is on
eating and drinking,
marrying and giving in marriage.

The idolatry here,
is the idolatry of the ordinary.

The life of the commonplace,
the life of comfort,
taking priority over the life of faith.

The gods of day to day
worshipped,
to the exclusion of the one true God.

And so,
they were not ready,
for God coming into their world.
Matthew's Gospel goes on
to tell several parables
of people not being ready.

Of those who got distracted by ordinary life while waiting.
The every day cares and worries,
the distractions and pleasures.

The owner of the house,
because of a good night's sleep
—not ready for the thief in the night.

Wicked servants,
hanging out with friends
—not ready for their master's return.

Bridesmaids,
napping
—not ready for the groom.

A slave,
too afraid of risk
to do something with the talent
he'd been given
—not ready for his master's call to account.

People,
too caught up in their lives
to notice the Son of Man
in the hungry,
in the thirsty,
in the stranger,
the one in need of clothing,
the sick one,
the prisoner.

Too focused
on themselves,
to feed, to clothe,
to welcome,
to care for, or to visit.

And therefore
—not ready for judgment day.

There is a word of judgment here.

For each one of these stories
judgment
upon the ones
who are not ready, who are not active,
who have nothing to show for themselves
for those who did nothing
who claimed they didn't know any better

They are left out,
they are excluded,
they are left behind.

We see that in our lesson today:
One will be taken.
One will be left.

But the ones
who are left behind here
in our lesson today
are just simply
—left behind.

Not for some coming punishment,

but to stay right where they are.
In that ordinary life,
working in the field
grinding meal.

The ones who are taken,
go somewhere new
—out of their ordinary life.

The word *taken*
means more like
"taken alongside of."

They go somewhere new with.

With the son of man.

They go with him on
to some new life
about which, we can only imagine.

• • •

Back to that pastor
I told you about
at the beginning of this sermon.

In that moment nearly twenty years ago,
I remember very clearly being
horrified by what he said.

I was so disappointed in him.
In his jaded attitude.
How little faith he had in his people!

It just seemed so wrong.

But as a parish pastor,
I've come to realize, again and again,
that he was not wrong.

People don't want
to bring their problems to church.

People want their faith community
to comfort,
rather than challenge,
to protect,
rather than push them,
to validate the concerns of ordinary life,
not critique them.

Pastors, too,
have that same deep desire
to have everything be fine,
to keep things normal.

Pastors themselves,
have plenty of ordinary cares of their own
—that tend to get in the way.

But along comes the Word of God,
saying,
what none of us want to be told.

Along comes the Word of God,
with the direct opposite
of what we want to hear
in this season.

When we are all so preoccupied
with eating and drinking,
with our families of birth and marriage,
with our celebrations,

—the Word comes rushing at us
like an unexpected flood,
destroying all in its wake.

In this season
when we are focused
on adding to our possessions,
getting more,

—the Word comes sneaking in
like a thief in the night,
threatening to take away
the things we treasure.

In this time of the year,
when we try to stuff in more
to our already packed schedules,

the Word comes swooping down unexpectedly into our day,
right in the middle of what we were doing.

And it might sound like bad news,
like nothing we want . . .

But understand this:
Christ does not come into our lives
to make minor adjustments,
to tweak and tinker with the way things are.

Christ comes into our world
to change absolutely everything.

That may not sound like good news
to those for whom
everything is pretty good already,

for those who are just fine staying

right where they are.

But for those who are awake
to the reality of this world's brokenness . . .

for those who are aware of how
desperately they themselves,
and this world needs Christ . . .

for those who are honestly praying
for the kingdoms of this world to be destroyed
and Christ's kingdom to come . . .

for those who are yearning to go
with Christ
wherever that may lead . . .

for those hoping for new life . . .

This is the good news.

Amen.

# Afterword

**Richard W. Voelz**

Rev. Dr. Richard W. Voelz is assistant professor of preaching and worship at Union Presbyterian Seminary in Richmond, Virginia. Formerly, he served as senior minister of the Johns Creek Christian Church (Disciples of Christ) in metro Atlanta, Georgia. His books include *Tending the Tree of Life: Preaching and Worship through Reproductive Loss and Adoption* and *Youthful Preaching: Strengthening the Relationship between Youth, Adults, and Preaching.*

• • •

*When you love the truth enough*
*You start to tell it all the time*

**David Bazan, "People"**

As a relatively new seminary professor who made the transition from weekly preaching to teaching in the fall of 2016, I've had occasion to think about the task of preaching as resistance. Each fresh news cycle has brought me to further reflection, sometimes wishing I could "jump back into the ring" momentarily to address one thing or another. I envision part of my task now to help preachers think about preaching in this environment when it is such a daunting task. Beyond the classroom, for some of the most difficult news cycles, I will open up my private messages on social media for those who need help in the process of writing or rewriting sermons, as the case may be. And whether they are seasoned preachers or those just finding their voices, it seems that the task of preaching resistance does not come without anxiety. What does one say? How does one say it in ways that will be received, especially if one serves a "purple congregation"[1] at best, rather than among a congregation filled with active "resisters"? These situations are nothing new. For some of us, the heavy atmosphere of our current context has always colored our ministries. I grew up in a more conservative (though not fundamentalist) tradition that I left while in seminary, but my home church ordained me to ministry right out of college. Ordained in the summer of 2001, I was working as a minister to children and youth as I began my seminary studies. So it was Fall 2001 when I began seminary and was working in a congregation. As I was sitting in the hallway preparing for my Old Testament Introduction class that first semester, a professor's radio was on and began reporting the World Trade Center attacks. This was the context of the very beginning of my ministry. And then the unending wars in Iraq and Afghanistan. And then Hurricane Katrina. The acceleration and proliferation of social media. And the financial crisis. And Newtown. And then Trayvon Martin. And Ferguson. And Mother Emmanuel in Charleston. And so much more. And now the rise of the 45th presidency and all that has come to be associated with it. And of course, in the midst of all that, the narrative of "mainline denominational decline." This was the context into which my own ordination came and in which my years of congregational ministry and preaching took shape. And it is the context into which my call to teaching preaching and worship at Union Presbyterian Seminary has come. Still, I cannot fail to mention the privilege I am afforded as a middle class, white, cisgender, heterosexual male. By virtue of my identity I have not encountered the kinds of discrimination and trauma many experience on a daily basis. But I cannot understate how this milieu has framed my own ministry, perhaps in differentiation from some of my older colleagues in ministry and academia who knew a different environment. I point to this to describe not just my situation, but the hyperawareness, hypersaturation, and urgency felt by those now daring to enter ministry and in which preparation for various ministries takes place. Pastors and congregations cannot get away from the racist, misogynistic, homophobic, transphobic, xenophobic, classist, nihilistic, creation-destroying, and fascist impulses in the United States. They shape daily (and often hourly!) life. Preaching takes place in the context of repeated trauma for individuals and communities. And as Phil Snider cites clergy colleague Elizabeth Grasham in the introduction, preachers are no longer able to even keep up with responding to each new element in the pulpit. There is no such thing as crisis preaching anymore, not when our contexts narrate to us an unending cascade of crises.

So how shall we preach faithfully? In response to the current context, Serene Jones observes, "If the church's message about God's love for the world is to be offered to those who suffer these wounds [of trauma], then we must think anew about how we use language and how we put bodies in motion and employ imagery and sound. With fresh openness, we must grapple with the meaning of beliefs not only about grace, but about such matters as sin, redemption, hope, community, communion, violence, death, crucifixion, and resurrection."[2]

I am glad to see the sermons in this volume. They are only a small representation of the kinds of preaching that occurs in pulpits across the United States. It seems that many preachers are taking the direction from Jones seriously, and in doing so, are giving fellow preachers and listeners the stuff of resistance. The times demand that we engage in this work. And I am glad to see the preachers here come from diverse communities.

Preaching that boldly resists the ugliest impulses and injustice we see across the U.S. landscape takes courage and exercises some sense of risk. But preaching as resistance cannot amount to a violent counterassault, especially not on the people who entrust us with the authority of the pulpit. I often tell my students that they cannot simply toss out "justice bombs" in the pulpit on Sunday morning and walk away, self-satisfied that they have done their duty. Resistance preaching is done gracefully, generously, and nonviolently, even as it does not back away from the kind of serious "public theological naming" described by Christine Smith of the kind of preaching that weeps, confesses, and resists.[3]

Phil Snider has rightly named three broad principles of resistance preaching in his introduction; I would like to name five more that I believe characterize the work throughout the sermons in this volume:

### 1. Resistance preaching requires an engaging, voiced vision of the kingdom of God.

Well before this current era, homiletician David Buttrick was preparing us for this time. And though he did not get the kind of attention that other homileticians of his era did, when they were largely focusing on sermon form, Buttrick offers a compelling cornerstone for resistance preaching. Writing in the late 1990s, Buttrick laments: "Somehow in the twentieth century the image of the kingdom of God seems to have disappeared. Oh, we still pray the great prayer, 'your kingdom come'; but if you ask Christian folk for definition of the phrase, most can only shrug. Is the kingdom of God merely a mythical alternative to our enlarging social discontent? The sense of a kingdom of God moving in our world with the awesome impetus of God's purpose has disappeared. . . . God is shaking the human world and calling us to do a new thing."[4] Critiques of the term "kingdom" notwithstanding, if preaching means to resist, it must take on the radical imagination of the kingdom of God expressed in the song of Mary and the ministry of Jesus of Nazareth.

### 2. Resistance preaching requires a community of support and a deep spiritual well.

One of the things that excites me about the sermons in this volume is that even in a loose fashion, it shows that there is a network of homiletic resistance. Because talking about the trauma that deeply affects us all can take a toll and because congregational reactions to resistance preaching can vary wildly, preachers need to know that they are not alone. You, preacher, are not alone. And be sure that in the process of preaching resistance, you find not only community but food for your soul as well. As is often said with regard to preaching, "You cannot give what you do not have." I believe you will find spiritual nourishment in the sermons collected here.

### 3. Resistance preaching requires historical consciousness.

We must disabuse ourselves of the notion that we are the first ones to engage in this work, as if we are doing something new. In preparing for the work of resistance, preachers should also surround themselves with "a great cloud of witnesses" who have resisted through their preaching. Whether that is the preachers of the Civil Rights era, those who resisted Hitler, abolitionist preachers, those who resisted Cold War and nuclear proliferation in the 1980s, or many others, we are not the first generation of resistance preachers. So it is important to know about, to read, and to listen to those who took to the "sacred desk" to preach resistance. They will have something to teach us about what to say and how to say it.

### 4. Resistance preaching requires a revised sense of authority.

As much as preachers seek to speak authoritatively, they will not do so in an authoritarian fashion, lest we fall into the rhetorical trap of mirroring those we seek to resist. Preachers will seek to listen, to engage in conversation, and to collaborate week in and week out. This is particularly the case if preachers recognize that they occupy privileged positions: seeking to listen and understand underrepresented and threatened groups must be part of the preaching task, before opening one's mouth to speak. Resistance preachers ask "How can I speak 'with' and 'on behalf of' others rather than 'to' and 'for'?" And in doing so, they bear witness to a different mode of authority.

### 5. Resistance preaching does not only say "no," but rather simultaneously says "no" and "yes."

Though not a preacher, Henry Giroux says that the work of educators should be "to make despair unconvincing and hope practical."[5] The work for resistance preachers is the same. We cannot simply preach against the -isms, attitudes, and institutions that work evil in the world. We are called to fight against despair's pretense to prevail through making hope both real and practical for our people beyond congregational worship. As Ruth Duck notes, a characteristic of Christian worship is that it functions as "rehearsal," which she means in both an eschatological sense and in the sense of a rehearsal for ethical living beyond the gathering of Christian worship.[6] The sermons in this volume exemplify inviting listeners to a better, more hope-filled way.

By way of concluding, I'd like to share a concern about preaching as resistance. As I write this, we are removed only one day from another deadly school shooting in Kentucky. And it has barely registered on the national scale in comparison to Oscar nominations. We're calling this "normalization." So my worry is not that preachers will lose their jobs for being too risky or confrontational. My worry is that resistance preaching will grow stale . . . that it will lose heart . . . that like our protesting feet and sign-holding hands, it will build up callouses.[7]

But here is my hope for preachers of the resistance: "when you love the truth enough you start to tell it all the time." The song lyric from David Bazan at the beginning of this essay suggests that preaching resistance begins with a love of truth that will not let us go and about which we cannot stop talking, perhaps like fire shut up in our bones. May it be so.

---

[1]I credit this term to Leah Schade, assistant professor of preaching and worship at Lexington Theological Seminary, and contributor to this book.

[2]Serene Jones, *Trauma and Grace: Theology in a Ruptured World,* 3rd ed. (Louisville: Westminster John Knox Press, 2009), 11.

[3]Smith, *Preaching as Weeping, Confession, and Resistance.*

[4]David Buttrick, *Preaching the New and the Now* (Louisville: Westminster John Knox Press, 1998), 1–2.

[5]Henry A. Giroux, *Teachers as Intellectuals: Toward a Critical Pedagogy of Learning* (Granby, MA: Praeger, 1988), 128.

[6]Ruth C. Duck, *Worship for the Whole People of God: Vital Worship for the 21st Century* (Louisville: Westminster John Knox Press, 2013), 14–16.

[7]Editor's note: in a tragic irony, I'm finishing my edits to this afterword on February 14, 2018, the same day as yet another mass shooting, this time in Parkland, Florida. Aric Clark's sermon, "When Thoughts and Prayers Turn to Ash," was a late addition to this collection that reflects on this tragedy (see chapter 14). This note is a haunting—and unexpected—conclusion to this book. May grace and strength and courage be with you as you preach in these times.

# MORE BOOKS YOU MIGHT LIKE

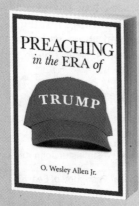
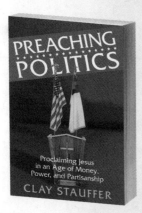